THE BOOK OF THE WILES OF WOMEN

Folio 63R—Madrid: Biblioteca de la Real Academia de la Lengua

UNIVERSITY OF NORTH CAROLINA
STUDIES IN THE ROMANCE LANGUAGES
AND LITERATURES
Number 27

THE BOOK OF THE WILES OF WOMEN

translated by
JOHN ESTEN KELLER

M L A TRANSLATION SERIES
NUMBER 2

CHAPEL HILL
THE UNIVERSITY OF NORTH CAROLINA PRESS

Copyright, 1956

The University of North Carolina Press

Presses of
The Orange Printshop
Chapel Hill, North Carolina

TO LOUISE AND OWEN KELLER,
MY PARENTS

FOREWORD

The present volume is the second in a series of translations published under the auspices of the Modern Language Association of America. The purpose of the series is to present to interested readers great works of foreign literatures done into English; it is hoped thereby to meet a need in university and college courses in such fields as comparative literature, world literature offered by English or Humanities departments, and individual literatures in translation offered by foreign language departments. Although the plan will remain flexible, the intention is not to duplicate standard items in existing publishers' lists. Such works as *Madame Bovary, Faust, Don Quixote,* and the *Divine Comedy* are easily accessible in authoritative translations and inexpensive editions. There are, however, important pieces of literature which cannot so easily be obtained because they do not appeal to the same large audiences. This new MLA Translation Series is concerned with fostering such works.

MLA Committee on Translations
C. R. Linsalata
B. Q. Morgan
Irving Putter

CONTENTS

Frontispiece

FOREWORD vii
INTRODUCTION 1
THE BOOK OF THE WILES OF WOMEN 14
NOTES 51
BIBLIOGRAPHY 57

THE BOOK OF THE WILES OF WOMEN

INTRODUCTION

ORIGIN AND DISPERSION OF TALES

THE EASTERN TALE has assumed from time to time a large number of different forms and has been the vehicle of almost countless plots, themes, and motifs; but the measure of its importance and greatness to western culture lies in its survival not only in literature but also among the folk. Tales of undeniably far-eastern origin live on today in such collections of stories as *Uncle Remus* and in other books made famous by their ancient anecdotal content. It is not unreasonable to state, then, that the tale is the Orient's greatest single contribution to the literature of the West. Benfey's school[1] went so far as to propose as dogma that *all* tales are ultimately of Indian origin, an idea that met with a great deal of opposition;[2] but even today, in spite of the loss of prestige suffered by this theory, every serious attempt to trace the sources of the *Märchen* or folktale must consider the theory of Indian derivation with care.

The Book of the Wiles of Women stands as a good example of the migration of tales from the Far East, because the majority of its stories probably had their beginnings in India.[3] At a time not precisely known these tales were assembled, linked together by means of a frame-story like beads upon a string, and read by Indians as a part of their literature. Polish and literary handling, however, cannot conceal traces of popular origin, and many of these tales, essentially unchanged, to this day form a part of the repertoire of oriental tale-tellers. Indeed, in altered form, yet with the essential plot elements intact, many of them survive in the literature and folklore of Europe; and some of the most refreshing renditions are to be found in the great Appalachian Mountain region of our own country.[4]

It is possible that some of the stories date back to a very ancient oral tradition, and that as folktales they entertained and helped to instruct the primitive Aryan tribes who wandered across Europe and Asia and whose language eventually blossomed into what is to us the most important of all language families. In India, it is believed, these tribes first attained a high degree of civilization and first developed a literature. In India the ancient tales made their debut in written form, where they became crystalized and static and where they were able to survive the vicissitudes and perils experienced by purely oral forms.

Among the best repositories of such tales and among the most influential upon the development of European prose fiction was the ancestor of *The Book of the Wiles of Women*. To this great work, which is no longer extant and the very title of which is not known, scholars have given various names,[5] but *The Book of Sindibad* is the most widespread and recurrent designation English-speakers have for it.

Benfey believed that all descendants of this book stemmed from a Sanskrit archetype, whose title, he suggested, might have been *Sindhapati*; but no trace of such a lost original has been discovered, nor is any exact date hazarded for its composition.[6] We know that the Buddhists, perhaps during the life of the Buddha (563?-483? B.C.), gathered many tales from the folk and employed them in preaching and teaching.[7] To the disciples of the Buddha the tales had considerable didactic worth, since they were interesting enough to catch and hold the attention of the simple people who were to be converted. Some 1500 years later European preachers re-discovered these values.

The long journey made by *The Book of Sindibad* from India to Western Europe has not been plotted with exactitude, nor have scholars succeeded in tracing and noting all the numerous changes undergone by the collection of tales in its westward passage. The many alterations that are known to have occurred in the stories as they made their way through various languages and cultures can give only an inkling as to the possible number of lost variants. Numerous versions of the extant tales, and even of the frame-story, indicate that changes were inaugurated with the intention of acclimatizing and adapting motifs to the several sets of national and cultural mores through which they passed.

The migration westward of another great collection, or at least of long and connected sections of it, has been more satisfactorily studied. This important set of stories is known as the *Panchatantra* (The Five Books). Among certain other affinities found in this collection and in the *Book of Sindibad* are tales common to both. Indications of this sort point to identical sources and a common *milieu*, and, in the opinion of many students, to routes of migration that closely coincided.

The date of the *Panchatantra* is usually given as the sixth century of our era, although quite possibly it existed, even in written form, a good deal earlier. A.D. 570 is the approximate date set for the translation of certain parts of this Indian work from the original Sanskrit into Pehlevi, the literary Persian of that time. This translation seems to have been made under the patronage of an enlightened monarch named Anuxirvan or Chosroes (ruled 531-579). The Pehlevi version unfortunately has passed into oblivion, but we know that it existed because the extant Arabic translation of it preserves even the long preface of the Persian Barzuyeh.[8] In the preface we read that this Persian, a physician of the king, journeyed to India in search of certain herbs that purportedly had the virtue of resuscitating the dead. As it turned out, the herbs stood allegorically for books of wisdom treasured by the Indians. When Barzuyeh returned to his king bringing the wonderful books that had the power of reviving, not actual corpses, but the intellectually and spiritually dead, the king sent him forth to teach their contents throughout the realm.

A noted Moslem intellectual named Abdallah-ben-Almocaffa[9] translated into Arabic the now lost Pehlevi rendition of Indian tales. As a writer and poet of renown and a recent convert to Islam, he was exceptionally well-qualified for his task; moreover, his name and political prominence must have focused the attention of erudite Baghdad upon the tales he translated and very probably did much to disseminate them across the Mohammedan world.

This Arabic version bearing the title *Kalilah wa Digmah* was finished about the year 750. It provided the linguistic connection necessary for the entry of the stories into a western culture, for it was through the Arabic that they made their way into Spain, then under Islamic domination. That the Spanish Moslems enjoyed these much-traveled tales is indicated by their longevity. They must have lived on in Spain for more than five hundred years, because it was not until the year 1251 that a translation of them appeared in Castilian at the behest of Prince Alfonso, who ascended the throne a year later as Alfonso X. The Spanish title was *Calila e Dimna* (Calila and Dimna), perpetuating, as did the Arabic, the names of two characters in one of the frame-stories. A Latin rendition by John of Capua appeared in 1270 with the title *Directorium Vitae Humanae*,[10] and by the end of the thirteenth century many individual tales from the collection had become current in the major languages of Europe.[11]

Such is the history of the Indian *Panchatantra*, or of those parts of it that reached Europe in the middle of the thirteenth century, and such probably is the history of *The Book of Sindibad*.

Just two years after the translation of *Calila e Dimna* from the Arabic, *The Book of Sindibad* also passed into Spanish as *El libro de los engaños e asayamientos de las mugeres* (The Book of the Wiles of Women).[12] This is the earliest extant translation of the eastern branch of the work into a western vernacular tongue, although certain of its better-known tales had been current from an earlier time in Europe, most often through the medium of Latin. Their presence in this tongue is attested in Aragon as early as the end of the first decade of the twelfth century in the *Disciplina Clericalis* of a Spanish Jew named Rabbi Moseh Sephardi and baptized Petrus Alphonsi.[13] From Spain the stories of the *Disciplina Clericalis* spread rapidly until they penetrated most of the languages of the West. So popular did his collection become that it must be considered one of the most important writings of the Middle Ages.[14]

THE SINDIBAD TRADITION IN EUROPE

Versions of the western branch of *The Book of Sindibad* had become established in Europe before the thirteenth-century Spanish rendition, and the development and dissemination of these versions in Europe and the Near East are pertinent to the appearance of *The Book of the Wiles of Women in Spain*, for they serve to throw a good deal of light upon the entry of the Sindibad tradition into that country.

The Sindibad tradition flowed into western culture in two separate currents, usually referred to as the eastern and western. To the eastern branch, which is the older and the more direct descendant of the lost original, belong seven important members, one of which is *The Book of the Wiles of Women*. The following is a list of the important surviving members of the eastern family:

1. The Greek *Syntipas*, late eleventh century, translated by Michael Andreopulos from a Syriac translation of a version written by Musa[15]
2. The Syriac *Sindban*, written between the middle of the eighth to the end of the eleventh century, from an unidentified Arabic version
3. The Persian *Sindibad-nâmah* (1375) in poetry, based upon a prose rendition of the twelfth century no longer extant

4. The Persian version of Nachschebi (d. 1329) that appears as the "Eighth Night" of his *Tûti-nâmeh*
5. The Hebrew *Mischlè Sendabar*, translated from Arabic probably in the first half of the thirteenth century
6. The Arabic version, which survives only in the episode of the Wazirs in *The Thousand and One Nights* of the fourteenth century
7. The Spanish *Libro de los engaños e los asayamientos de las mugeres* (*The Book of the Wiles of Women*), translated (1253) from an unidentified Arabic version.[16]

The western branch, thought to have been put together first in Byzantium, is really an offshoot of the eastern. Any of several of the eastern versions could have been its immediate source, but it has closer affinities with the Hebrew than with the other existing texts. Whatever its genesis may have been, the western branch differs so radically from all the members of the eastern branch that it must have separate treatment and classification. Nearly all the details, motifs, and even the stories that in the eastern branch serve as points of contact and relationship are absent.

Pilgrims returning from the Holy Land, or perhaps Crusaders or merchants, could have carried the western branch of tales into Europe. As it moved westward it divided into two separate currents of its own: the version known as *The Seven Sages*, according to Krappe,[17] was assembled first by a northern Frenchman (ca. 1135) from folktales brought home from the East by the men of the First Crusade; the version called the *Dolopathos* was made known generally to Europe in the Latin rendition of Johannis de Alta Silva,[18] probably in the late twelfth century. Both of these currents of the western branch penetrated most European languages, and Spain has three examples from the version of *The Seven Sages*, all of a late date: *Novella que Diego de Cañizares de latyn en romance declaro e traslado de un libro llamado "Scala Çeli"* (fifteenth century), *Historia de los Siete Sabios de Roma* (1530), and *Historia lastimera del Principe Erasto* (1573).[19]

The present study has been confined primarily to the development of the eastern branch, the ancestor of *The Book of the Wiles of Women*. Professor Jean Misrahi treats the western branch in his work, *Sept Sages* (Paris, 1933), and Professor Urban T. Holmes, Jr. presents a study of this branch in *History of Old French Literature* (New York, 1937).

PRINCE FADRIQUE'S BOOK

The Book of the Wiles of Women opens with a preface which gives the reason for its composition. From this preface we learn that Prince Fadrique of the royal house of Castile caused the book to be translated from Arabic into Spanish in the year 1291 of the Spanish *Era*, 1253 of our own.[20] How widely this translation was read, what influence it exerted upon the development of Spanish prose fiction, and which Spanish writers drew directly from it will probably never be known. No actual mention of its title is made in any Spanish writing until in 1863 Amador de los Ríos made it known to the world in his *Historia crítica de la literatura española* (III, 536-541); but certain of its individual tales appear in later Spanish works of the Middle Ages[21] and the Renaissance, as well as in more modern periods. Two are contained in the *Count Lucanor* (mid-fourteenth century) of Don Juan Manuel, Fadrique's nephew; and Archdeacon Clemente Sánchez de Vercial included several in his *Book of Exempla by A.B.C.* (first quarter of the fifteenth century). These two collections of tales may have drawn upon other sources than Prince Fadrique's book, for other sources were available, both literary and popular. It is quite possible, however, and even probable, that a book of stories translated from the Arabic at a time when interest in Islamic literature was high, under the patronage of the brother of King Alfonso the Learned, in one of the medieval world's greatest centers of intellectual activity, may have attracted and captured the notice of the erudite of the day and may have made itself felt in their writing.[22]

As one of the purest surviving representatives of the ancient Sindibad tradition and of the peculiar syntax and vocabulary of thirteenth-century Spain,[23] *The Book of the Wiles of Women* holds today a place of note in the literary production of that formative period of Hispanic culture.

ANALYSIS OF "THE BOOK OF THE WILES OF WOMEN"

King Alcos[24] of Judea was so perturbed by his inability to beget an heir that he could not sleep. One night his favorite wife came to him with a pious suggestion. She told him to pray to God, asking him for a son. In due time a son was born to them, and every preparation was made to make his reign successful. When the court astrologers came to cast the infant's horoscope, their findings were alarming. The prince would have a long life and a happy one, they predicted, if he could avoid a great danger that would threaten him in his twentieth year. Alcos placed the prince under the tutelage of a wise man named Sindibad (in Old Spanish Çendubete) who promised to teach him in six months what no other sage could teach him in sixty years. As it turned out, he kept the boy a number of years. The day before the prince was to return, educated, to his father, Sindibad cast his horoscope and discovered that the danger foretold at the young man's birth was at hand. He found that if the prince should speak during the next seven days, grave peril would result. The prince promised to remain silent and returned mute to the court to the consternation of the king, while Sindibad wisely went into hiding for seven days.

One of the prince's stepmothers, a young woman and Alcos' current favorite, took the prince to her apartments, nominally to draw him out of his silence. Instead she suggested that they murder Alcos, marry, and reign jointly. Furious and outraged, the young man forgot his promise to Sindibad and threatened to expose her at the end of seven days. Realizing that her life depended upon removing the prince before the allotted time expired, the woman accused him of attempting to violate her. Alcos was enraged at his son, and, urged on by her insistence that justice be done, ordered the execution of the prince; but seven sages, counselors of the king, decided that they must delay the sentence. They knew that the king, in a repentant mood, would blame them for failing to advise him properly. In an effort to save the prince, each of the sages related two tales (except the third sage, who told only one) to convince Alcos that the woman was lying and that his son was innocent.

Of the thirteen tales told by the sages, nine portray the wiles of women, three the danger of unpremeditated action, and one, rather inconsistently, the wisdom of a virtuous wife. The stepmother told stories on alternate days, stories intended to reveal the wickedness of men, in particular of the advisers of kings. While this battle of stories raged, the life of the prince hung in the balance, since the king was persuaded by each tale, pardoning or condemning his son after each. Finally on the eighth day the prince spoke, exposing his stepmother's perversity, and told five tales to convince the assembled wise men of the kingdom that Sindibad's teaching had been successful. At this, Sindibad returned from hiding to be rebuked mildly by Alcos, then heaped with rewards and honors. The king ordered the wicked stepmother burned to death in a dry cauldron.

This Spanish work follows the general pattern of all the versions of the eastern branch of the tradition. It is the only member, however, that names a king of Judea, and is one of the three in which the woman is executed.

PREVIOUS TRANSLATIONS

In 1868 the Instituto Lombardo in its transactions for the year published an edition of *El libro de los engaños* by Domenico Comparetti, who made it from a handwritten copy of the original manuscript sent him by Amador de los Ríos. This edition was far from perfect. Of greater value was the study of the Sindibad tradition that accompanied it. The study by Comparetti, entitled *Ricerche intorno al Libro di Sindibâd*, was translated into English in 1882 for the Folk-Lore Society as *Researches Respecting the Book of Sindibad*. With it appeared a translation of *El libro de los engaños* made by a Mr. Coote. This translator apparently misunderstood certain constructions in the Spanish of the thirteenth century, left several long and extremely difficult passages entirely out of his work, and deleted whole sentences on the grounds that they were unseemly or incoherent. "I have omitted this unimportant part," he wrote (*Researches,* p. 121, note), "where the Spanish text is hopelessly corrupt." And again: "I have purposely abridged my translation for obvious reasons." (p. 136, note.)

It seems, therefore, time to publish a second and modern translation, complete and unhampered by Victorian niceties out of place in the mid-twentieth century. Using my own edition of *El Libro de los engaños* (Chapel Hill, 1953), I have rendered the language of Prince Fadrique's Spain into present-day English, have included every passage, and have not altered the meaning, I believe, in any way. The word *e* ('and') has been omitted when used excessively and needlessly in the original, and synonyms have been substituted for the literal translation of *dixo* ('he' or 'she said'), which was the only word employed to describe speech in *The Book of the Wiles of Women*. Since the original text carried no punctuation, the necessary punctuation marks have been inserted.

FUNCTION OF FADRIQUE'S BOOK IN MEDIAEVAL SPANISH SOCIETY

The purpose stated in the dedication, that is, that the book was composed and translated to alert men against the wiles of women, can hardly be taken seriously. Everthing in the actual content of the work indicates that it was put together for entertainment, though a didactic reason may have been given, tongue-in-cheek, for added levity. Surely no one who reads the tales today can seriously consider them didactic, nor is it easy to believe that the Spaniard of the thirteenth century found them less amusing than we. Present-day readers react, of course, in various ways, but to some the frame-story itself is packed with drollery. To these the actions of King Alcos, seesawing ever between death and reprieve for his son, motivated solely by the outcome of a series of tales, is more than mildly amusing. Might not this have struck Alfonso's courtiers similarly? Others, however, find nothing laughable in the behavior of this Alcos, hot with righteous anger against a would-be violator of the family's sanctity, yet able to repress his emotions and postpone his vengeance while the stigma of dishonor lingered on, all for the sake of hearing another tale. To these the didactic note rings true.

Be that as it may, even if we accept the avowed didactic purpose of the book, among readers at King Alfonso's court as among those in Araby, Persia, and Ancient India, these merry, lively, piquant, and sometimes unrestrained tales also spelled diversion. A Spanish sentiment unfavorable to detailed pornography raises them far enough above their Arabic counterparts—often very lewd and vulgar when measured by occidental standards of decency—to render them acceptable to our modern tastes; but whether refined in form and handling or not, the stories are enjoyable.

TALES AND EXEMPLA

Moralized tales, even some of those found in *The Book of the Wiles of Women*, had been employed at various periods in Asia to teach lessons of a practical, if not of an ethical nature in solving life's problems. Didacticism under Christianity aimed at guidance of a completely diffrent kind. How surprising it is, then, to read some of the raciest accounts of marital infidelity among the sermons of the Church during the thirteenth, fourteenth, and fifteenth centuries. A case in point is the story of the weeping bitch related by the fourth sage in *The Book of the Wiles of Women*. This oriental tale, borrowed from the Sindibad tradition by the *Disciplina Clericalis* and spread by this Latin work, appears as *Exemplum* 339 in a collection of tales written and alphabetized for preachers in need of illustrative anecdotes for sermons.[25] The archdeacon who assembled these tales was innocent, we believe, of trying to be indecorous. He was fol-

lowing the tradition of using *exempla*. According to the rules
of this tradition any sort of tale was proper so long as it could
be made to support a moral. If it could be made interesting
enough to command the attention, its value increased enormously.
Didacticism and interest served to strengthen one another.

The title of each of the accounts in *The Book of the Wiles of
Women* includes the word *enxenplo* which I have translated simply 'tale,' 'account' or 'story.' To mediaeval man the Latin word
exemplum was a tale whose moralization was clearly and unmistakably stated in support of some exposition. From the
fourth century until the end of the fifteenth the genre of the
exemplum increased in popularity and importance until it became
the vehicle of most of the short prose narrative in Europe. Its
role in the development of the tale and in the dissemination and
preservation of motifs can hardly be overemphasized, and a brief
examination of its flowering in connection with Prince Fadrique's book will be helpful.

Investigations of the *exemplum* in European literature reveal
that these tales with clearly stated moralizations drew from a
multiplicity of sources. Any theme—literary, popular, historical,
legendary, religious, secular, ancient, modern, contemporary
with the times, profane, or sacred—could become an *exemplum*
by having a moral lesson appended.

Centuries before the coming of the oriental tale the Church
had used *exempla*. Indeed, the very word was an ecclesiastical
usage, and great success in teaching the simple and uneducated
was attributed to this form. At first, themes from Scripture and
stories, often miraculous, concerning the saints and the early
Fathers of the Church formed the background for *exempla*. When
these themes grew worn and repetitious, the clergy looked about
for fresh ones, since it had been discovered that only through
stories could the laity of the times be instructed with any facility.[26]

Well-known names stand out as advocates of the use of *exempla*. St. Ambrose (304?-397) used them and wrote urging
their employment. He believed that they could sway people much
more effectively than words and he recommended that preachers
follow his example, using them often.[27]

In the fifth century St. Augustine (345-430) urged the use
of *exempla*, related them himself, using as sources the Bible, the
lives and miracles of the saints, elements of the already large

and growing body of Christian legend, material from antiquity, and his own personal experiences. He told interesting little anecdotes about people that he knew, and concluded such accounts with a few lines of practical wisdom and a moralization.

A century later Pope Gregory the Great (540-604) gave the *exemplum* its greatest impetus. By using *exempla* in his homilies, endorsing their efficacy, and by writing his *Dialogues*, a treatise which is really a collection of *exempla*, this great man established the moralized tale as a fixed form for homiletic literature. His conviction that men could learn more from the experiences of other men than from dry precept was of great moment to the later development of narrative prose. The eight *exempla* in his *Dialogues* soon spread the length and breadth of eastern and western Christendom and exerted a mighty and lasting influence upon all the collections of monkish tales that were to increase and multiply with such fecundity for the next 800 years. Even though the invasions of barbarian tribes held back the progress of learning, and therefore of the *exemplum*, for several centuries, the writings of Gregory were not lost. Their pattern endured. The importance of these writings can hardly be overestimated, since nearly all collections utilized the *Dialogues* and borrowed from them heavily.

The seventh and eighth centuries brought more in the way of new materials to the *exemplum*. In Spain St. Isidore of Seville (560-636) in his *Etymologies* employed anecdotes and mythological treatises, some of which were to appear from time to time in collections of *exempla* as a means of enlivening texts. The process continued until in the twelfth century the moralized tale came into wide use and in the thirteenth and fourteenth centuries reached the peak of its success.

So it was that the Church, through its preachers and doctors, developed the *exemplum* as a didactic device, never quite losing sight of the interest value inherent in such stories. And so it was that many a theme alien to the Faith crept into homilies, instruction books, and even sermons. Carried by the clergy, these reached to the ends of the Church's empire.

The preaching friars furnished the most important medium for the dissemination of tales. Vying with minstrels and jongleurs, these ubiquitous clerics gathered tales, some of them scurrilous, and liberally sprinkled their sermons with them. Preaching suddenly changed its character and received a new

and enormously stimulating impulse in the founding of two
great religious orders, the Franciscans (founded in 1208) and
the Dominicans (1216). Since poverty was one of the vows of
both orders, their members came in direct contact with the low-
liest and most despised of social classes, a matter of signal importance to the *exemplum* and to the very style of story telling,
as well as to preaching. With such audiences and congregations,
crude and completely untutored, elements of pungent interest
had to be present.[28] These two great orders journeyed over
Europe, the Near East, and parts of Africa, preaching to the
ignorant in the vernacular, bringing with them the moralized
tale as one of their principal attractions. With these they
frightened, instructed, praised, and captivated the people who
listened. Franciscan and Dominican collections of tales, and
later collections made by other orders, appeared in French,
German, Italian, Spanish, English and other national tongues.
Works of important collectors were taken everywhere, and the
old favorite sources continued to hold their own beside the
newer oriental material coming into use. It was due to the
friars that many *exempla* were translated into the vulgar languages. Spain possessed some of the best and most extensive
collections to be found in European literature.[29] In medieval
Europe the friars, without being aware of it, had restored to the
tale the ancient didactic role it played among the Buddhists so
many centuries before.

Prince Fadrique's Book of *enxenplos* or tales represented the
purely recreational role of the *exemplum*. Since each tale car-
ries a moralization of sorts—if one may thus describe the way
each tale repeats the reason for its telling, i.e., to teach the wiles
of women to unwary mankind—it came technically under the
classification of *exemplum*. But the intent, possibly farcical,
of being didactic carried a hollow ring, and *The Book of the
Wiles of Women* is simply a collection of entertaining short stories. Another cycle was complete, for the very tales that had
delighted the courts of Baghdad, medieval Persia, and ancient
India were exercising the same function in Castile.

As short stories the *"enxenplos"* of Spanish literature had a
great vogue, reaching the apogee of literary perfection and ex-
cellence in the perennially celebrated *Count Lucanor* of Don Juan
Manuel (1282-1348) and in the not yet fully appreciated *Book
of Exempla by A.B.C.*, set down by the Archdeacon of Valderas.
Boccaccio saw the wealth that lay in the same oriental sources

drawn upon earlier by Petrus Alphonsi and in his own time by Don Juan Manuel, Juan Ruiz, Archpriest of Hita, and Chaucer. The eastern tale in its best literary aspects had made itself at home in the West.

As true *exempla*, however, these tales and most of the other themes found in treatises and sermons fared less prosperously. There had been objections quite early to their professedly pious exercise: scabrous, licentious, even blasphemous ideas reached the people from the pulpit itself; stories were told that dealt with matters best left unmentioned, and people might actually learn sin through hearing tales intended to illustrate its punishment;[30] the tales were being told *per se* because their telling made the people laugh, and preachers related them as they saw fit, often in a manner unseemly; through such wrongful use of *exempla* the Church herself was losing heavily in dignity. John Wycliffe in England fulminated against the employment of narrative material in sermons;[31] readers of *The Divine Comedy* will recall what Dante had to say about the irreligious use of *exempla* in the preaching of his time;[32] the Church Councils of Salzburg (1386), Sens (1528), Milan (1565), and Bordeaux (1624) issued decrees ever more threatening against the use of *exempla* by preachers.[33]

In spite of, perhaps even because of, so much antagonism,[34] pious *exempla* lingered on in written, and later in printed collections, as well as in sermons. The Church was never able to suppress the moralized stories it had taught the people to love and expect. Changing styles, not the Church, brought to a close the vogue of monkish tales, the new learning made mock of them, and the tradition, more than a thousand years old, of the true *exemplum* with all the name implies, withered.

The Book of the Wiles of Women, often listed as a group of *exempla*, was actually not of the legitimate variety: its morals are all suspect; its tales overshadow didactic purpose; it does not come up to the specifications of didacticism. It survives because it never succumbed to all the canons and formulae of the genuine *exemplum* and because basically most of its stories arose from the folk.

THE BOOK OF THE WILES OF WOMEN

PRINCE FADRIQUE,[35] son of the very noble and blessed King Ferdinand[36] and of the most holy and virtuous Queen Beatrice, through whom he could never lose his fine name, heeding the words of the sages to the effect that good repute never dies for him who does good works and that nothing is more advantageous than knowledge for winning everlasting life, turned his mind to the path of learning. He took a ship outfitted for the sea, a ship upon which he risked no danger in journeying into everlasting life. Now mankind, since life is fleeting and since knowledge is strong and enduring, cannot learn or understand anything more. Through love, learning, and doing good works to those who love him, everyone learns what is bestowed upon him and sent down from above. The prince considered it meet and was pleased to have this book translated out of Arabic into Castilian to forewarn those deceived by the wiles of women.[37] This book was translated in the year 1253.

There was once a king of Judea whose name was Alcos. He was a mighty monarch and he greatly loved the people of his kingdom, ruling them ever with justice. He had ninety wives, and although he had known them all in accordance with his faith, in none could he beget an heir. As he lay one night with one of them, he began to worry about who was to inherit the realm after his death. Pondering this, he grew sad and tossed in his bed in extreme despondency.

At this time one of his wives, she whom he loved the most, came to him. She was prudent and wise, and he had tested her in certain matters. She came to him because she saw that he was unhappy and she told him that he was honored and loved by his people throughout the land.

"Why are you so sad and despondent?" she asked. "If you are afraid of something, or if I have grieved you, let me know in what way, and I will mourn with you. If it is something else, you shouldn't worry so much, for thank the Lord, you are loved by your subjects and all speak well of you and with affection. May God never sadden you and may you have His blessing!"

"Pious and beloved one," said the king to his wife, "you have never failed to comfort me and to lighten my care when I was sad; but neither I with all my power nor all the people of my kingdom can assuage this sadness that besets me. I should like to leave an heir who would inherit the realm when I die. That is why I am sad."

"I shall give you a good piece of advice," said his wife. "Pray to the Lord, who is all-virtuous, for He is powerful enough to create a son for you and to send him to you. He has never tired of bestowing grace, and you have never asked for anything that He didn't give it to you. When He understands that you pray in earnest, He will give you a son. I think it proper, if it is in accord with your wishes, that we arise and pray with all our hearts that He give us a son in whom we may rejoice and who may become our heir. I believe firmly that He, in his kindness, will grant it to us if we beseech Him. If he sends us a son, we must be happy and must obey His will, be satisfied with His justice, and appreciate His grace, because God is omnipotent and everything rests in His hand. He takes unto Him whomever He will and He smites whomever He wishes."

After she had told him this, the king was pleased, for he realized that all she said was true. They both arose and prayed as she had suggested; and after they returned to bed, Alcos lay with her and filled her with child.

As soon as they knew positively, they praised God for the kindness He had done them. Nine months later she gave birth to a healthy son, and the king rejoiced exceedingly and was greatly pleased with him. And the woman praised God for it.

Then the king summoned all the sages that were in his kingdom to come before him to study the horoscope of his son. When they arrived, he was glad to see them and he caused them to come into his presence.

"Welcome!" he said.

And he was with them for a long time, rejoicing and making merry.

"I declare to you, Sages," he said, "that God, whose name be praised, has favored me with the gift of a son, whom He bestowed upon me to strengthen my arm and to make me happy. Let thanks be given to Him forever! Examine my son's star and learn what his fate will be."

They studied it and informed him that his son's life would be long and that he would be very powerful; but that at the end of his twentieth year something would happen to him, in dealing with his father, through which he would be in mortal peril.

When the king heard this, he was frightened and filled with

grief, but he grew happy again and said, "Everything is in God's power. Let Him do what He thinks meet."

Now the prince matured and grew tall and handsome, and God endowed him with great intelligence. In that entire age no other was born his equal. When he was nine years old, the king sent him to learn to write, and he studied until he was fifteen; but he learned nothing, and when the king heard this, he was quite concerned.

He sent for all the wise men of the kingdom. When they all had arrived, he addressed them. "What do you think of the case of my son? Isn't there one of you who can teach him? I will give that one anything he asks, and he will have my everlasting affection."

Then four of the wise men present—nine hundred were there —stood up, and one of these said, "I shall teach him so that no one will be wiser than he."

"Why didn't you teach him?" the king asked a wise man whose name was Sindibad.

At this they all spoke, and afterwards Sindibad said, "Is that all you know? Well, I know all that and consider it little, for nobody is wiser than I. I will teach him. Grant me what I ask, O King, and I shall teach him in six months so much that no one will be wiser than he."

"He who speaks and does not accomplish," replied one of the four, "is like a flash of lightning with no rain. Why didn't you teach him anything in the years you had him with you, while the king was supporting you?"

"Because of the great pity I felt for him I could not drive him," answered Sindibad, "and because I was trying to find someone wiser than I. Now I realize that no one knows better than I how to teach him."

"There are four things," retorted the second sage, coming to his feet, "which a wise man should not praise before he sees their final outcome: the first is food, until we see what becomes of it after it has been digested by the stomach; the man who goes forth to battle, until he returns from the army; the crop until it is harvested; and the woman until she is pregnant. Therefore, we ought not to praise you until we see why we should. Let us see your hands accomplish something and let us hear your mouth say something that will make known your wisdom and your intent."

"He who has his hands and his feet under control," said Sindibad, "and his hearing, and his sight, and his whole body, is like that wisdom which rules the mind. Just as musk permeates water and fills it with sweet savor, so wisdom in the heart makes the whole body sound."

"One who doesn't learn in infancy," asserted the third sage, "places in his mouth what his stomach will cast up. A woman can never be good when she has no fear of her husband. A man who speaks wisdom, if he doesn't understand and know what it is, never imparts any meaning to the one who hears him, nor does he himself comprehend it. And you, Sindibad, since you were unable to instruct the boy in his infancy, how can you teach him when he is of age?"

"You will see," replied Sindibad, "if God wills and if I live, that I shall teach him in six months what no one else can teach him in seventy years."

"Let me inform you," said the fourth sage, "that when wise men assemble, they meet one another, they debate with one another, and yet they do not understand the wise things they say to each other. Will you do what you say? I want you to prove how you can do so."

"I shall show you," answered Sindibad. "I shall teach him in six months what no one else can teach him in sixty years, in such a way that no one will know more than he, and I shall not delay an hour, because they have convinced me of these things: that in a country where the royal authority is also the judicial and does not dismiss men legally after trial, where it is known that there is no law to correct what the king has done when under the temptation of wealth, that the situation is similar to that of the physician who is so fond of his holidays that he doesn't call upon the sick as they believe he should. If such a state of affairs prevails in a kingdom, one ought not to live in it. Now that I have revealed all this to you, I shall also inform you that kings are like fire; if you go too near, you will be burned, and if you stand apart, you will be chilled. I request, Sire, that if I teach your son, you will give me what I desire."

"Demand what you will," replied the king, "and if you will not ask, I shall act for you, for there is nothing worse in kings than deceit. Tell me what you want."

"That you will not do to anyone what you do not want anyone to do to you," answered Sindibad.

"I promise," said the king.

They made a contract, and both agreed upon a month and upon the hour of the day that it was to terminate. They wrote in a formal agreement all that was necessary for that day.

During the second hour of the day Sindibad took the boy by the hand and led him to his house where he had prepared a great hall, marvelously beautiful. He wrote upon the wall all the sciences the boy was to learn, all the stars, all the formulae, and all the other things.

"This is my chair," he told the boy, "and this is yours until you learn all the knowledge that I learned in this room. Cheer up! Sharpen your wits and your ears and your eyes!"

He sat down to teach him, and what they had to eat was brought there to them; they did not go out and no one visited them there. Now the boy was keen and intelligent, and before the appointed time arrived he had learned all the facts that his master, Sindibad, had written about the wisdom of mankind.

The king inquired about his son two days before the day designated. When his messenger arrived at Sindibad's house, he said, "The king wants you to come to him immediately."

"Sindibad," demanded the king, "what have you accomplished? What news do you have?"

"Sire," answered Sindibad, "I have news that will please you, for your son will be with you tomorrow two hours after dawn."

"Sindibad," cried the king, "a man like you never broke his promise. Consider yourself in high honor, for you deserve to have a reward from us!"

Sindibad returned to the boy and said, "I shall cast your horoscope."

He cast it and saw that the boy would be in mortal danger if he spoke before the passage of seven days. In great distress he said to him, "I am greatly disturbed on account of the contract I signed with the king!"

"Why are you distressed?" inquired the boy. "For if you ordered me never to speak, I would never speak. Tell me what you want, for I will do it."

"I made a promise to your father," said Sindibad, "that you would return to him tomorrow, and I must not fail in the agreement that I made with him. When two hours of the day have passed, go to your father, but do not speak until seven days have gone by. In the meantime, I shall hide."

When the next day dawned, the king had the people of his kingdom regaled with food and he had platforms erected to seat the minstrels who were to play before them. Then the son came to his father. The king went to him and greeted him, but the boy did not reply. This the king considered strange.

"Where is your master?" he asked the boy.

Then the king ordered a search made for Sindibad, and heralds went forth to look for him. They searched far and wide but could not find him.

"Perhaps," remarked the king to those who were with him, "the boy is in awe of me and is afraid of me and does not dare to speak."

The king's counselors all spoke to the boy, but he made no reply. Then the king said to those who were with him, "What do you think is the matter with my son?"

"It seems to us," they replied, "that Sindibad, his teacher, has given him something, some drug to make him learn, and the drug has rendered him mute."

And the king considered this of great import and he grieved exceedingly.

THE STORY OF THE WIFE AND HOW SHE TOOK THE PRINCE
ASIDE IN HER APARTMENT, AND HOW, BECAUSE OF WHAT
SHE SAID TO HIM, HE FORGOT WHAT HIS TEACHER HAD
TOLD HIM

The king had a wife whom he loved and honored above all the wives he possessed. When they told her what had happened to the boy, she went to the king and said, "Sire, they have told me what has happened to your son. Perhaps through embarrassment in your presence he doesn't dare to speak. If you agree, let me take him aside, and perchance he will tell me what is the matter, for he used to tell me his secrets, a thing he never did with any of your other wives."

"Take him to your apartment and talk to him," said the king.

She did so, but the prince did not answer anything she asked him. Then she pressed him further, saying, "Don't be a fool, for I know well that you won't oppose my will. Let's kill your father. You will be king and I shall be your wife, for your father is quite old and weak. You are a young man and your life is just beginning and you ought to expect a great deal more than he."

As soon as she had said this, the boy was furious and he

forgot what his teacher had told him, all that he had commanded him.

"Ah, Enemy of God, if the seven days were but passed I would give an answer to what you say!" he cried.

He had no sooner said this than she realized she was in danger. Screaming and calling for help, she began to tear her hair, so that the king, hearing her, wanted to know what was the matter.

"This one," she lied, "who you say cannot speak, tried to violate me utterly, and I would never have thought it of him!"[38]

On hearing this, the king flew into a great rage and cruelly ordered the boy executed. Now the king had seven privy-counselors without whose advice he never acted. When they saw that the king had ordered his son put to death without having consulted them, they understood that he did so in wrath because he believed what his wife had told him. They took counsel together and said, "If he kills his son, later he will be sorry, and will blame nobody but us; hence we must give some reason for the sparing of the prince."

"I will excuse you all from the embarrassment of speaking with the king," said one of them.

This counselor went straight to the king, fell upon his knees before him, and said, "Sire, man should never do anything until he is certain. If you do so, you will commit a wrong. I shall tell you, by way of example, the story of a king and of one of his female subjects."

"How was that?" asked the king.

The wise counselor spoke, "I have heard it said that there was a king who loved women, and this was his only fault. Now this king, standing one day upon a lofty housetop, saw below him a very beautiful woman, and he was enamoured of her. When he sent to ask her to come to him, she replied that she could not, since her husband was in town. As soon as the king learned this, he sent her husband off to war.[39]

"Then the wife, who was chaste and pure and very wise, said to the monarch, 'Sire, you are my king and I your slave. Whatever you desire, that I desire; but I must go bathe and make myself ready.'

"After she had returned, she handed one of her husband's books to the king, a book in which were laws and judgments as to how adulterous women are mocked. 'Read this book, Sire, while I make myself beautiful.'

"The king opened the book and found in the first chapter how adultery should be forbidden, and he was greatly shamed, and what he had wanted to do weighed heavily upon his soul. Putting the book on the floor, he hastened through the door of the house, leaving his sandals forgotten beneath the couch upon which he had been sitting.[40]

"A little later the husband returned from the army. As soon as he sat down, he suspected that the king had slept there with his wife and he was terrified, not daring to say anything through fear of the king, and not daring to live with his wife.

"This state of affairs lasted some time, and the wife told her people that her husband had left her and that she did not know why.

"'Why,' they queried, 'do you no longer go to your wife?'

"'I found the king's sandals in my house,' he told them, 'and I am afraid. That is why I don't dare to see her.'

"'Let us go before the king,' they said to him, 'and let us give him a parable, but let us not reveal the case of your wife. If he is quick-witted, he will understand it.'

"They went before the monarch and said to him, 'Sire, we have a field which we gave to this good man to till and cultivate and enjoy the fruits thereof. He worked it for a while and then he deserted it.'

"'What do you say to this, good man?' asked the king.

"'They were right when they stated that they gave me a field. But one day when I went into the field, I found the footprint of a lion and I was afraid that he would devour me. For this reason I stopped tilling the land.'

"The king spoke to him, saying, 'Verily, the lion entered the field, but he did there nothing to harm you, nor did he bring any evil upon you. Go back, therefore, to your land and cultivate it.'

"And the good man returned to his wife and asked her what had taken place, and she told him everything truly as it had happened. He believed her, because of the statements made by the king, and had greater faith in her than ever before."

THE TALE OF THE MAN, HIS WIFE, THE PARROT, AND THE SERVANT GIRL[41]

"Sire, I have heard that a man was most jealous of his wife. He purchased a parrot and placed it in a cage in his house, commanding it to tell him all that it saw his wife do, concealing nothing. Later he went about his business. His wife's paramour then went to her in her room, and the parrot saw everything that they did there. When the husband returned from his business, he sat down in his house without his wife's being aware of his presence. He had the parrot brought in and he questioned it as to what it had seen. The parrot told him all that it had seen his wife do with her lover, and the husband was furious at her and no longer lived with her.

The wife thought that certainly the servant girl had betrayed her, and she summoned her and said, 'You told my husband what I did!'

The servant swore that she had not told him, saying, 'But it was the parrot.'

At nightfall the wife went to the parrot and put it on the floor. Then she poured water over it as if it were raining. She took a mirror in one hand and a lamp in the other, one below the cage and one above. The parrot thought it was lightning. The woman began to turn a large grindstone, and the parrot believed it was thunder. All through the night until dawn came the woman did this.

When it was morning, the husband came and asked the parrot, 'Did you see anything last night?'

'I could not see anything,' replied the parrot, 'because of the downpour that fell and because of the lightning.'

'If all you have told me about my wife,' said the husband, 'is as true as this, nothing in the world is as false as you, and I shall have you killed.'

Then he sent for his wife, pardoned her, and they made peace.

And, Sire, I have not related this fable to you for any reason except that you may understand the deceits of women, whose wiles are potent and numberless."

And the king ordered that his son should not be killed.

THE ACCOUNT OF HOW THE WIFE CAME ON THE SECOND DAY BEFORE THE KING AND TOLD HIM IN TEARS THAT HE SHOULD PUT HIS SON TO DEATH

"Sire," she said, "you ought not to pardon your son, because he has done something worthy of death. If you do not kill him, and let him live after having committed such a wicked deed, no one will hesitate to do likewise. I am going to tell you, Sire, the story of a launderer and his child."[42]

"How was that?" inquired the king.

"There was," she related, "a launderer who had a small son. This launderer, when he had to wash clothes, took his child with him. When the boy began to play in the water, the father never attempted to correct him and there came a day when the boy fell into the water. When the father jumped into the water to save the son, they both sank. And, Sire, if you do not see to the punishment of your son before he commits further atrocity, he will destroy you."

And the king ordered his son put to death.

OF HOW THE SECOND COUNSELOR WENT BEFORE THE KING TO SAVE THE PRINCE FROM DEATH

The second privy-counselor went before the king, knelt to him, and said, "Sire, if you had many sons, you shouldn't wish to kill any of them; but since you have only one son and you order him put to death before you know the truth, you are going to regret it sorely when you can no longer bring him back. Yours will be like the case of the merchant, his manservant, and the damsel."[43]

"How was that?" asked the king.

"Let me tell you, Sire, that there was a very rich merchant who was most finical in his eating and drinking. He went on a business trip and took a servant lad with him, and one night they lodged in a very fine city. The merchant sent his lad out to purchase food, and the lad met a damsel in the market place with two loaves made of prime wheat flour. Attracted by this bread, he bought it for his master and took it to him.

The merchant was extremely pleased with the bread and he said to the boy, 'For heaven's sake buy that bread for me whenever you can find it!'

Each day thereafter the lad went to the damsel and bought bread from her for his master; but one day he found that the girl had no bread and he returned to his master and told him. The merchant told him to ask the girl how the bread was made, and the lad went to look for her.

'My dear,' he said, when he had found her, 'my master wants you to do something for him.'

She went to him and said, 'What is your pleasure?'

'Damsel,' inquired the merchant, 'how do you make that bread? I want to have some made like it.'

'Good Sir,' she replied, 'some pustules broke out on my father's back, and the doctor told us to take the finest wheat flour and to knead it with butter and honey and to put it on those pustules. He told us to remove it after we had cleansed away and dried up all the pus. I took the dough and in secret made bread of it.

Then I carried it to the market to sell, and I sold it. And, praise God, my father is now well and we have stopped making the dough.'

The merchant uttered loud cries of loathing and disgust about that bread he had been eating, and seeing that there was nothing he could do, he fell to berating his lad, crying, 'Wretch! What shall I do? Let us find something with which to wash our hands, and our faces, and our mouths, and our feet, and our bodies. How can we cleanse them?'

And, Sire, if you kill your son, I fear that you will repent even as the merchant repented. Sire, don't do something which you will regret until you are positive about it!"

THE STORY OF THE MASTER AND THE MANSERVANT, OF THE WIFE AND THE HUSBAND, AND HOW THEY ALL FOUND THEMSELVES TOGETHER[44]

"Sire, people have told me about the wiles of women. They say that there was a wife who had as a lover one of the king's privy-counselors who held the whole city in fief from the hand of the king. Now this woman's lover sent a manservant to her house to find out if her husband was at home. When the servant entered the house, she was taken with him, for he was handsome, and he with her. She invited him to lie with her and he did so. Now the paramour, seeing that his servant was slow in returning, went to his mistress' house and knocked.

'What will become of me?' cried the manservant.

'Go and hide in that alcove,' she commanded.

The servant's master entered just then, and she did not want him to go to the alcove where the young man was hiding. Just then her husband knocked at the door.

'Draw your sword,' the woman instructed her paramour. 'Stand there at the door of that room and threaten me. Then, without saying a word, be on your way.'

He did so, and she went and opened the door for her husband, who, when he saw the man with the drawn sword, said, 'What is this?'

The paramour said not a word to him and departed. Then the husband turned to his wife and cried, 'Ah, you sinner! What business did that man have here who just went out insulting and threatening you?'

'The young man in that alcove,' she replied, 'came fleeing in terror from him, and finding the door unlocked, he came in crying for help, with his master on his heels ready to murder him. He ran to me, and I stood in front of him and prevented the man from killing him. That is why the man left here insulting and threatening me. But as God is my witness, he didn't frighten me!'

'Where is the young man?' asked the husband.

'He is in that alcove.'

The husband went to the door to see if the young man's master had gone away, and not seeing him about, he called the fellow and said, 'Go on out, for your master has departed.'

Quite satisfied, the husband turned to his wife and said to her, 'You played the role of a fine woman and you have done well, and I am very grateful to you.'[45]

And, Sire, I told you this story only so that you would not execute your son on the word of a woman, for in women are contained deceits without number."

And the king ordered the execution stayed.

THE ACCOUNT OF HOW THE WIFE CAME BEFORE THE KING ON THE THIRD DAY, TELLING HIM TO PUT HIS SON TO DEATH

On the third day came the woman, weeping and making moan before the king, saying, "Sire, these privy-counselors of yours are evil, and they will harm you just as a privy-counselor once harmed his king."

"How was that?" inquired the king.

"There was a king," she told him, "who had a son who loved exceedingly to hunt. The privy-counselor prevailed upon him to ask his father to give him permission to go hunting. Side by side they went, the prince and the privy-counselor, and a stag leaped away before them.

'After him until you catch him! Kill him and take him to your father!' urged the privy-counselor.

The lad rode after the stag until he lost his hunting party, and riding along, he came upon a path where he found a damsel weeping.

'Who are you?' asked the prince.

'I am the daughter of the king of such-and-such a land,' the damsel said, 'and I was traveling with my parents on an elephant. I went to sleep and fell off without my parents' seeing me. When I regained consciousness, I did not know where to go, and I lost the way as I followed them.'

The lad took pity on her and put her behind him on his mount. Traveling thus, they entered a deserted city.

'Let me down here,' said the damsel, 'for I have need. I'll come back shortly.'

The lad did so, and she went in among the buildings and stayed a long time. When he realized that she was late, he dismounted, climbed a wall, and saw that she was a ghoul and that she was there with her kin.[46]

'Go along with him to another ruin,' they were saying to her, 'until we can overtake you.'

Hearing this, the lad was terrified. He descended from the wall and jumped upon his horse. The damsel overtook him and rode behind him again, while he shook with fear of her.

'What makes you shake so?' she queried.

'I am afraid of my companion, for I fear that evil will come to me from her.'

'Can't you protect yourself with your wealth, since you have boasted that you are a king's son and that your father is so rich?' she jeered.

'I have nothing,' he answered.

'But you vaunt yourself as the son of a king and a great prince,' mocked the ghoul. 'Pray God to help you against your companion and you will escape.'

'That is the truth, and so I shall do. O, Lord God!' he cried, 'I beseech and plead that by Your Grace you free me from this devil and her people!'

Down toppled the ghoul and began to wallow on the earth, trying to rise and being unable to do so. Then the boy rode as fast as he could until he reached his father, and he was athirst and terribly frightened by what he had seen.

And, Sire, I have related this tale to you so that you will not depend upon your wicked counselors. If you do not wreak justics for me on the one who has wronged me, I shall destroy myself with my own hands."

And the king ordered his son put to death.

THE THIRD COUNSELOR'S STORY ABOUT THE HUNTER AND THE VILLAGES[47]

Then came the third privy-counselor before the king. Kneeling before him, he spoke. "Sire, great harm stems from things when a man doesn't weigh them. Such is the tale of the hunter and the villages."

"How was that?" asked the king.

"I have heard it said that a hunter coursing through the forest came upon some honey. He put it in a bag that he kept with him for carrying his water. Now this hunter owned a dog which he took with him. The hunter carried the honey to a village lying near the forest to sell it. Upon opening the bag so as to show the honey to the shopkeeper, a drop of honey fell out and a bee lighted upon it. Now the shopkeeper had a cat, and this cat leaped upon the bee and killed it; the hunter's dog fell upon the cat and killed it; the cat's owner came and killed the dog; and then the dog's master slew the shopkeeper. At this, the men of the shopkeeper's village came and slew the hunter, owner of the dog; finally, the men of the hunter's village marched against those of the shopkeeper, and they fell upon one another and all were killed, not even one remaining alive. So all were slain for one drop of honey.

"And Sire, I have related this tale to you so that you will not execute your son until you know the truth, and will not be sorry."

THE TALE OF HOW THE WIFE CAME AND TOLD THE KING TO KILL HIS SON, AND RELATED THE TALE OF THE KING'S SON AND OF HIS PRIVY-COUNSELOR, AND OF HOW HE BETRAYED HIM[48]

"There was a king," said the woman, "who had a privy-counselor and a son. He betrothed the son to the daughter of another king. Now the father of the princess sent a message to this king, saying, 'Send your son, and we will have him marry my daughter. Afterwards I shall send you notice of it.'

The king caused his son to be outfitted handsomely, and he sent him off to his wedding. Likewise, the monarch sent the privy-counselor with his son. As they rode along conversing, they drew away from their companions and came upon a spring which had the virtue of changing any man who drank of it into a woman. This power the privy-counselor knew, but he did not reveal it to the prince.

'Wait here,' he told the boy, 'until I go to find the way.'

He found the way, and he followed it and came to the boy's father.

'How is it that you are here without my son? What has become of him?' the king asked, badly frightened.

'I believe that wild animals have devoured him,' replied the counselor.

Now when the prince concluded that the counselor was slow

in returning for him, he went down to the spring to wash his hands and face. He drank of the water and was changed into a woman. Then his state of mind was such that it left him unable to decide what to do, or where to go, or what to say.

Just then a demon came up to him and asked him who he was.

'I am the prince of such-and-such a country,' said the lad.

The boy gave him his true name and informed him of the perfidy done him by his father's privy-counselor. And the demon pitied him because he was so comely.

'I will turn into a woman, just as you are, and at the end of four months I shall assume my own form again,' he said.

The prince listened to him, and they swore an oath upon it, but the demon returned in the form of a woman pregnant.

'My friend,' he said, 'change your form again as you were before, and I shall assume my former shape.'

'How so?' replied the prince, 'for when we took the oath and vow, I was a damsel and a virgin, and now you are a pregnant woman.

The prince argued the case with the demon before his infernal judges, and they decreed that the prince should win the case. Then the prince was changed into a man and he went after his wife, took her home to his father's house, and told him how it had all come to pass. The king ordered his counselor put to death for deserting the young man at the spring.

And I trust that God will aid me against your wicked counselors!"

The king ordered his son executed.

THE ACCOUNT OF THE FOURTH PRIVY-COUNSELOR ABOUT THE BATHHOUSE-KEEPER AND HIS WIFE[49]

Then came the fourth counselor before the king. Kneeling before him he said, "Sire, no man should ever do anything until he is absolutely positive of the truth, for anyone who acts before he knows the truth, errs just as a bathhouse-keeper who was sorry when it was too late."

"How was that?" asked the king.

"Sire, there was a prince who went one day into a bathhouse. He was a young man, but he was so fat that he couldn't see his own members. When he undressed, the bathhouse-keeper began to sigh and to shed tears.

'Why the tears?' inquired the prince.

'Because,' he replied, 'of your being the king's son, his only son, and not being potent as other men are, for upon my word I don't believe that you are able to have intercourse with a woman.'

'What shall I do,' asked the prince, 'for my father wants me to marry? Please take these ten *maravedis* and find a beautiful woman for me.'

Now the bathhouse-keeper said to himself, 'I shall keep these ten *maravedis* and shall send my wife to him, for I am perfectly confident that he is unable to lie with her.' Then he went to get her, and the prince lay with her.

He began to peep and to watch how the prince was getting along with his wife. And the prince laughed at him, and he was ashamed.

'Go home!' he roared at his wife.

But she replied, 'How can I go home? I promised him I would sleep with him all night long.'

Upon hearing this, out of anguish and grief, the bathhouse-keeper hanged himself and died. And, Sire, I told you this tale only so that you would not execute your son."

THE TALE OF THE MAN, HIS WIFE, THE OLD WOMAN, AND THE SHE-DOG[50]

"Sire, I have heard that a man and his wife took an oath of loyalty and fidelity. The husband swore to return by a certain date, but he didn't. The wife went out one day to the street, and while she was there, a man saw her and was smitten with her and he asked for her love. She told him that she couldn't and that she wouldn't for anything.

The man then approached an old woman who dwelt nearby and he told her all about how he had fared with that woman. He begged her to get the woman for him and promised that he would give her whatever she wanted. The old woman told him she was willing to do so and that she would obtain the woman for him.

Going to her own house, she took honey and dough and pepper and kneaded it all together and made bread of it. Then she started for the house of the wife, calling after her a little dog she had, and tossing pieces of the bread to it so that the wife didn't notice. As soon as the dog had eaten the bread, it commenced to follow the old woman, fawning upon her so as to get more of the bread, and shedding tears because of the pepper that was in it. When the wife saw the dog in such a state, she was astonished.

'Old woman,' she asked, 'have you ever seen any other dog weep like this one?'

'She does so with reason,' answered the old woman, 'because this dog was once a woman, and very beautiful, and she used to live near me. A man fell in love with her, and she was not interested in him. He put a curse upon her, that man who was in love with her, and she was changed instantly into a she-dog. Now, whenever she sees me, she remembers it and bursts into tears.'

'Woe is me!' cried the wife. 'What shall I do? Just the other day a man saw me in the street and asked to be my lover, and I refused. Now I am afraid he will change me into a dog if he curses me! Go to him quickly and plead with him, and I will give him whatever he wants!'

'I shall bring him to you,' said the old woman.

She arose and went out to look for the man. The wife went to beautify herself and then hastened to the old woman's house to see if she had located the man.

'I can't find him,' said the old woman.

'What shall I do, then?' asked the wife.

The old woman went out and found a man and said to him, 'Come here, for I have a woman who will do anything for you, anything I ask her to.'

Now this man was the woman's husband, but the old woman did not know it.

'What will you give to one who gets you a fine room, and a beautiful woman, and good food and drink, if you want it?' she asked.

'Heavens! I would like that!' he cried.

She led the way, and he came close behind her. When he saw that the house was his own, he suspected that she was taking him to his own wife and he imagined that his wife acted in this fashion whenever he went away.

'Come in,' said the evil old woman. 'Sit here.'

When his wife beheld his face and saw that he was her husband, she knew nothing to do but to carry the attack to him.

'So, Mr. Whoremonger!' she cried. 'Is this the faith you and I swore to keep? Now I know that you frequent bad women and wicked procuresses.'

'Woe unto you!' roared her husband. 'What are you trying to put over on me?'

'They told me,' answered his wife, 'that you were coming

home, and I made myself beautiful and told this old woman to go out and test you to see if you went with bad women. And I see that right away you desired a prostitute! Never more will we live together and you will never touch me again!'

'May God forgive me,' cried the husband, 'and so may you! I thought only that she was leading me to my own house and to you, and it grieved me terribly when she brought me here. I thought that you had been doing this with other men.'

The instant he said this, she tore her face and gashed it with her nails, crying, 'Now I see well enough what you thought of me!'

She raved at him, and when he saw how angry she was, he began to coax her and to plead with her to pardon him; but she refused to forgive him until he had promised her, as a gift, a village that he owned.

And, Sire, I gave you this story only to point out to you the perfidy of women, which is boundless."

THE ACCOUNT OF HOW THE WOMAN CAME ON THE FIFTH DAY AND TOLD THE TALE OF THE PIG AND THE APE[51]

On the fifth day the woman came and said to the king, "If you do not give me satisfaction against this prince, you will see what these wicked counselors will do for you. After I am dead we shall see what you will get from their advice. And when you stand before God, what will you say, having committed such a great wrong in letting your son live and having refused to see justice done? And how can you, failing to do what is just in this world, permit him to live, on the recommendation of your wicked advisers and privy-counselors? I know that you will be called to account by God! Now I am going to tell you what happened to a pig because of an ape."

"How was that?" asked the king.

"I say, Sire, that there was a pig that used to lie under a fig tree, eating the figs that fell to the ground. One day he went there to eat and found that an ape was up there eating figs. Now the ape, seeing him below, tossed him a fig. He ate it, and it tasted better than the ones he was accustomed to find on the ground. He lifted his head to see if the ape was going to throw any more to him, and he stayed waiting on the ape until the veins of his neck dried up and he died from it."

After he had heard this, the king feared that she would take the poison she was carrying in her hand, and he ordered his son slain.

THE FIFTH COUNSELOR'S TALE OF THE DOG, THE SERPENT, AND THE BABY[52]

The fifth counselor came into the king's presence.

"May God be praised!" he said. "You are wise and moderate and you realize that if anything is done in haste, before all the facts are known, it is done badly, and that if such a thing is done, it is done foolishly, and that when one wants to make amends, he cannot. And what once happened to the owner of a dog will happen to him."

"How was that?" asked the king.

"Sire," he said, "I have heard that there was a man who was the servant of a king. This man had a hunting dog, a good and intelligent dog, and it always did whatever he ordered it to do. It happened that one day the man's wife had to visit her relatives and that her entire household went with her.

'Stay with your son who is asleep in his crib,' she said, 'I shan't be away long and I shall be back in a hurry.'

The man sat down by his son, and while he was there a fellow came running from the king, saying that the king wanted him to come quickly.

'Watch out for the child, and don't leave him until I return,' the man told the dog.

The man closed the door and went to the king. While the dog was lying by the child, there came a large serpent, which, attracted by the odor of mother's milk on the baby, tried to kill him. As soon as the dog caught sight of the snake, he sprang upon it and tore it to pieces. Because of the love the man bore his son whom he had left alone, he returned quickly. When he opened the door, out came the dog to be praised by his master for what he had done, and upon his muzzle and chest was the blood of the serpent. The man thought, when he saw this, that the dog had killed his son, and drawing his sword, he smote the dog and killed it. Then, going to the bed, he found the child sleeping beside the mutilated body of the snake. When he understood all this, he beat his face and tore it, and he could do nothing more. He considered himself unlucky and knew that he had made a mistake.

And Sire, don't let such a thing happen to you in this matter, for afterwards it will be too late to repent. Do not execute your son, for the deceits of women are boundless."

THE STORY OF THE WOMAN AND THE PROCURESS, OF THE MAN AND THE MERCHANT, AND OF THE OLD WOMAN WHO SOLD THE CLOTH[53]

"Sire, I heard that there was a man who, whenever he heard women mentioned, went wild with the urge to possess them. He heard about a beautiful woman and he went to look for her and found where she was. Then he went to a procuress and told her that he was dying for that woman.

'You are wasting your time in coming here,' the old procuress told him, 'for she is a good woman, and you might as well not expect anything from her.'

'Get her for me,' he said, in spite of this, 'and I will give you whatever you want.'

The old woman promised to do so if she could.

'But you go,' she said, 'to the woman's husband, who is a merchant, and try to buy a piece of cloth that he has under the counter.'

He went, therefore, to the merchant and asked him to sell it to him; but he had a difficult time persuading him to sell it. He took it to the old woman, and she burned it in three places.

'Wait here in my house so that nobody will see you,' she told him.

She took the cloth, folded it, hid it under her cape, and went to see the merchant's wife. While she was talking to her, she concealed the cloth under an ottoman and then departed. When the merchant came in, he picked up the ottoman to sit on and he found the cloth and believed that the man who had bought it was his wife's lover and that he had forgotten to take the cloth away with him. He arose and beat his wife badly, giving no reason, and went off with the cloth in his hand. His wife covered her head and went to her father's house.

When the old woman heard this, she went to see her and said, 'Why did your husband beat you so for nothing?'

'I don't know,' replied the wife. 'In all truth, I don't!'

'Some spell-binders have worked evil against you,' the old woman told her. 'But, dear, do you want me to tell you something? In my house is one of the wisest men in the world, and if you will come there at vespers with me, he will tell you what to do.'

The good woman said that she wanted to come. Vespers arrived, and the old woman came for her and took her with her to her house and put her in the room where the man was. And he arose and lay with her, and the woman, through fear and shame, was silent. But after the man had lain with her she went off to her kinsmen.

And the man said to the old woman: 'I am very grateful for this and I shall give you something.'

And she replied: 'Don't worry about this, for I shall make good what you have done. Make your way slowly past the house of her husband. When he sees you he will call you and ask you about the cloth and what you have done with it. You tell him that you sat down near the fire and that it was burned in three spots, that you gave it to an old woman so that she could mend it for you, and that you haven't seen it since and don't know anything about it. And I shall walk slowly past that place, and you say, "I gave the cloth to that one." And you call to me and I shall explain everything away for you.'

Then he went and found the merchant.

'What did you do with the cloth that I sold you?' he asked.

'I sat down near the fire,' he replied, 'and I didn't notice, and it was burned in three places. I gave it to an old woman, a neighbor of mine, so that she could mend it, and I haven't seen it since.'

While they were discussing it the old woman arrived, and the man called her and said to the merchant, 'This is the old woman to whom I gave the cloth.'

The merchant called her and asked her what she had done about the cloth.

'Upon my word,' she answered, 'as God is my witness, this young man did give me a piece of cloth to mend, and I went with it under my cloak into your house, and honestly I don't know whether it was dropped in your house or in the street.'

'I found it,' said the merchant. 'Take your cloth and go your way in peace.'

The merchant then went home and sent for his wife at the house of her parents and begged her to forgive him, and she did so.

And Sire, I told you this tale so that you would understand the deceit in women which is vast and limitless."

THE TALE OF HOW THE WOMAN CAME ON THE SIXTH DAY AND TOLD THE STORY OF THE ROBBER AND THE LION, AND HOW HE RODE HIM[54]

The woman came on the sixth day and said to the king, "I trust in God who will shelter me from your wicked privy-counselors, as He protected a lion on one occasion."

"How was that?" asked the king.

"Once a great caravan was passing close to a village," she said. "A thief, a very great evildoer, entered the caravan. Now as they were traveling, night overtook them and a hard rain fell upon them.

'Watch your things,' cried the caravan leader, 'so that no wicked robber will do us harm!'

At that very moment the robber went in among the beasts, unnoticed because of the extreme darkness. He began to feel to see which was the largest animal so that he could steal it. Now he put his hands upon a lion and found that no other was as large or as thick at the neck, and he mounted the lion.

'This is the fiend that men talk about,' thought the lion. And he ran the whole night until morning.

When they saw each other, they were terrified. The weary lion came to the foot of a tree, and the man seized a branch and climbed into the tree for fear of the lion. The lion fled in terror and met an ape.

'What is the matter, lion?' asked the ape.

'Last night,' cried the lion, 'the fiend took me and rode me until morning. He never tired of riding me!'

'Where is that fiend?' inquired the ape.

And the lion showed the ape the man in the tree, and the ape climbed up into the tree, while the lion watched carefully to see what would happen. The ape saw that it was a man and made a sign for the lion to approach. The lion came running. Just then, the man climbed down a bit, grasped the ape by the genitals, and squeezed until he had killed him. Then he threw him down to the lion, at which the lion fled, crying, 'May God be praised, for I have escaped from this fiend!'

"I am confident," continued the woman, "that God will aid me against your wicked privy-counselors, just as He helped the robber against the ape."[55]

And the king ordered his son put to death.

THE TALE OF THE COUNSELOR ABOUT THE DOVE AND THE DOVE'S MATE THAT STORED UP WHEAT IN THEIR NEST[56]

The seventh counselor came, knelt before the king, and said, "If you had no son, you ought to beg God to give you one. How, then, can you put to death this son that God has bestowed upon you? For if you slay him, you will suffer evil from it, just as the dove suffered."

"How was that?" asked the king.

"Sire, a dove and his mate dwelt in a forest and had their nest there. Now in August they gathered their wheat and stored it in their nest. The dove went away on a trip and ordered his wife not to eat a single grain of wheat while summer lasted.

'But go,' he said, 'to the fields and eat what wheat you find there, and when winter comes, you will eat this wheat and enjoy it.'

Afterwards came the season of great heat, and the grain shriveled and decreased in quantity.

'Didn't I command you not to eat a grain of wheat and to save it until winter?' cried the dove on his return.

She swore that she had not eaten a grain, not even a particle. But the dove preferred not to believe her, and he began to peck her and to strike her with his wings until he killed her. Then the dove noticed the wheat and saw that it was swelling in the dew and that there was no more nor less than before. And he was distraught because he had killed his mate."

THE TALE OF THE MAN AND HIS WIFE AND OF THE ROBBERS WHO TRICKED HER[57]

"Sire, I heard a story told about a man and his wife. They dwelt in a village, and the man used to go out to plow. The wife cooked him a loaf of millet bread and carried it to him where he was plowing. As she was going along carrying it to him, robbers fell upon her and snatched away the bread. One of the robbers made a figure of an elephant, in mockery, and put it into the basket without her seeing it. They released her, and she went on to her husband. When he opened the basket, he saw it.

She looked and saw what the robbers had done.

'I dreamed last night while I slept that you were before a tailor who grieved you sorely. Then I went to some men so that they might interpret this dream for me, and they told me to make a figure of millet and have you eat it and that you would be saved from anything that might happen to you.'

The husband said that this dream could be true.

Such is the deceit and such the wiles of women—boundless."

THE TALE OF HOW THE WOMAN CAME ON THE SEVENTH DAY BEFORE THE KING, COMPLAINING AND SAYING THAT SHE WANTED TO BE BURNED. AND THE KING QUICKLY ORDERED HIS SON SLAIN BEFORE SHE COULD BE BURNED

When the seventh day came, she said, "If this youth does not die today, I shall be discovered! Nothing is left for me except death."

She gave everything she had to the poor, had a great deal of firewood brought, seated herself upon it, ordered the fire lighted all around, saying that she wished to be burned. When the king heard it, before she could be burned, he ordered his son put to death.

The seventh privy-counselor appeared, placed himself between the youth and the one who was to kill him, made obeisance before the king, and said,"Sire, do not slay your son on the word of a woman, for you do not know if she is lying or is telling the truth. You had such a great yearning to have a son, as you know, and God caused you to be happy. Do not bring Him grief."

OF THE TALE OF THE SHE-DEVIL, THE MAN, AND HIS WIFE, AND OF HOW THE MAN REQUESTED THE THREE GIFTS[58]

"Sire, I have heard that there was a man who never lived apart from a she-devil and that he had a child by her. One day it came about that she wanted to leave him.

'I fear that I shall never see you again,' she told him, 'but I want you to learn three prayers from me, so that when you ask God for three things, you shall have them.'

Then she revealed to him the prayers and departed. The man, very sad over the departure of the she-devil, went to his wife and said to her, 'Know that the she-devil I had has left me and that I am awfully sad. I had many good things from her. She has revealed to me three prayers with which I can ask three things from God and can have them. Now you advise me so that I can have these things from Him.'

'You know perfectly well that you men love women and delight in their favors,' said his wife. 'So beg God to give you women.'

Now when he saw himself burdened with them, he cried out to his wife, 'God confound you, for you brought this about with that advice of yours!'

'Don't you still have two prayers left?' she asked. 'Beg the Lord to rid you of these women, since you are having such a hard time with them.'

He repeated the prayer, and they all vanished. Then he began to curse his wife.

'Don't curse me,' she cried, 'for you still have another prayer. Ask God to make everything just as it was before.'

And all was as before. So he lost all the prayers.

Therefore, I advise you not to slay your son, for the evils of women have no end. On this subject I shall give you a story."

"How was that?" asked the king.

THE TALE OF THE YOUNG MAN WHO DID NOT WISH TO MARRY UNTIL HE HAD LEARNED ALL THE EVILS OF WOMEN[59]

"Sire, they have told me that a man didn't want to marry until he had learned and discovered the evils of women and their wiles. He traveled until he arrived at a village where they told him that wise men dwelt, very deeply versed in the wiles of women, and that it would cost him dearly to learn their arts.

The one there who was the wisest said to him, 'Do you want me to tell you something? You will never know nor will you ever completely learn the deceits of women until you sit for three days upon an ash heap and eat nothing except a little barley, bread made of barley, that is, and a little salt.'

He answered that it was agreeable to him. Then he seated himself upon the ash heap and transcribed many books about the arts of women. After he had done so, he said that he wanted to return to his own land. He lodged in the house of a good man, and the host asked him all about himself. He told the man from whence he had come, and of how he had sat upon the ash heap while he transcribed those books, and of how he had eaten the barley bread, and of how he had endured a great deal of hardship and wretchedness, writing about the arts of women.

When he had finished speaking, the good man took him by the hand and led him to his wife, saying, 'I have a good man who comes weary from travel.'

And he told her his business and begged her to take him in charge until he was stronger, since he was weak. Having told her this, the husband went about his business. Now the wife knew perfectly well what she would teach him. She questioned him as to who he was and what was his business, and he told her everything. When she understood all this, she took him for a booby and a simpleton, for she was well aware that he would never finish what he had set out to do.

'I firmly believe,' she told him, 'that no woman in the world will ever deceive you, nor will one ever be the equal of those books you have composed.' But in her heart she said: 'Be as wise as you may, for I shall make you see this stupidity of yours under which you labor. I am just the woman who knows how to show you!'

Then she called him and said, 'Friend, I am a young woman and beautiful and I am ripe, and my husband is a tired old man. It has been a long time since he lay with me. If you want to, lie with me, since you are a smart fellow and full of experience. But say nothing to anybody!'

When she had spoken, he believed that she was in earnest. He stood up and tried to take her in his arms, but she said, 'Not so fast! Let's undress.'

He stripped, and she began to scream and shriek. The neighbors came running, and before they entered she told the fellow, 'Stretch out on the floor. If you don't, you are a dead man!'

He did so, and she placed a large bite of bread in his mouth. When the neighbors came in, they asked what had happened.

'This man is our guest,' she replied. 'He almost choked on a piece of bread and his eyes have rolled back in his head!'

Then she showed him to them, and she poured water upon him to revive him. He gave no signs of revival during all this while she was pouring cold water upon him and washing his face with a napkin. Finally, the men left and went about their business.

'Friend,' said the woman, 'in your books are there any arts like this one?'

'By my faith, never did I see one nor did I ever find one like this in my books!' he answered.

'You endured hardship and bad days for nothing,' she told him. 'Never expect anything else from all that, for what you sought you could never have, neither you nor any man alive!'

When he realized this, he took all his books and cast them into the fire, admitting that he had wasted his time.

"Now Sire, I have told you this story so that you will not kill your son on the word of a woman."

And the king ordered them not to execute his son.

OF HOW ON THE EIGHTH DAY THE PRINCE SPOKE AND WENT BEFORE HIS FATHER

When the eighth day came, early in the morning before the sun rose, the prince called the woman who was serving him during those days when he was not speaking.

"Go and call So-and-So, who is privy-counselor to the king," he ordered her, "and tell him to come as fast as he can."

As soon as she saw that the prince was speaking, the woman went running and called the privy-counselor, who arose and came quickly to the prince. He wept with him and told him why he had not spoken and what had happened to him with his step-mother.

"And I did not escape death except through you and your companions, who strove to help me out of justice and loyalty. May God reward you for it, and I shall give you a reward if I live and learn what you desire. Now I want you to hasten to my father and tell him my tidings before that false whore, my step-mother, goes to him, for well do I know that she is an early riser!"

As soon as the prince had spoken, the privy-counselor went with all speed to the king.

"Sire!" he cried. "Reward me for the news I bring about the good and the mercy that God has done you because you didn't kill your son. He now speaks, and has sent me to you."

He did not tell the king all that the prince had said.

"Go quickly and tell the prince to come to me immediately," commanded the king.

He came and made obeisance, and the king asked him, "What was the matter with you that you didn't speak to me in the face of death?"

"I shall tell you," said the prince.

He told it all to him, how it had befallen him and how his master, Sindibad, had forbidden him to speak for seven days.

"But I tell you that the woman took me aside and tried to instruct me. When she learned that I couldn't answer for seven days, she had no other plan than to make you put me to death before I could speak. Therefore, Sire, I beg you, that if you consider it a good thing, you have all the wise men of the realm and of your peoples assemble, for I should like to speak before them all."

When the prince had spoken, the king was very happy.

"God be praised," he cried, "for all the good He has done me! He did not permit me to commit such a great error as to put my son to death."

The king had his people summoned to court. When they had arrived, Sindibad came in to the king and said, "Sire, I bow before you."

"What became of you, wicked Sindibad, during all these days?" asked the king. "I was on the point of killing my son because of what you told him to do!"

"God shed so much grace upon you," answered Sindibad, "and so much prudence and understanding, that you had to act as you did when you knew the truth. You kings, above all men, ought to be most certain of the truth. The prince did not fail to do what I commanded him to do. You, Sire, should not have ordered him slain on the word of a woman!"

"Praised be God that I did not put my son to death," cried the king, "for I would have lost this world and the next! Now, you Sages, who would have been to blame had I executed my son? Would the blame have been mine? My son's? My wife's? The teacher's?"

Four sages stood up, and one of them said, "When Sindibad examined the boy's star and what his fate was to be, he should not have gone into hiding."

"It is not as you say," said another sage, "for Sindibad was not at fault, because he had made a contract with the king which he could not break. The fault must be the king's, because he ordered his son put to death on the word of a woman, when he did not know if her story was true or false."

"It is not as you say," said the third sage, "for the king was not to blame, because in all the world there is no wood colder than sandalwood, nor anything colder than the clovepink,[60] yet when they are rubbed together, they will generate so much heat that fire will come forth. Now, if the king had been wise in his judgment, he would not have been swayed by the will of a woman; but since she was the woman the king loved, he could not help listening to her. The fault lay with the woman, because she deceived him with her words and caused him to order his son slain."

The fourth sage said that the blame was not the woman's, but the prince's, because he refused to keep secret what his master had commanded him to.

"For the woman," he said, "after she realized how handsome and well-made the prince was, desired him all the more when she had him alone with her.

"Now when she understood what the prince was saying, she knew that she would be discovered at the end of the seven days by what the prince would say. She was afraid that they would execute her, and therefore she took pains to have him put away before he could speak."

"It is not as you say," stated Sindibad, "for the greatest of all wisdom lies in speaking."

"I shall speak, if you command me," the prince said.

The king told him to say what he wished.

"Praise be to You, O God," exclaimed the prince, getting up, "Who caused me to see this day and this hour! Who permitted me to make known my story and my mind! It is necessary that I reveal my thoughts, for I wish to demonstrate my wisdom and to tell you a tale about it."

THE TALE OF THE MAN, OF THOSE WHOM HE INVITED, OF THE MAIDSERVANT WHOM HE SENT AFTER MILK, AND OF THE SERPENT THAT DROPPED THE POISON[61]

The sages asked him to speak, and he said, "They say that a man prepared a feast and invited his guests and his friends, and dispatched his maidservant to the market for milk for them to drink. Now she purchased it and was carrying it home on her head. Above her a kite flew and it was carrying in its claws a serpent which it squeezed so tightly that the venom ran out of it and fell into the milk. They drank the milk and all of them died from it. Now tell me whose fault it was that all of those people perished?"

"The fault," replied one of the four sages, "was the host's, because he didn't examine the milk he gave them to drink."

"You are mistaken," said another sage, "for hosts can't look at everything and taste everything that they have served: the fault was in the kite that squeezed the serpent so hard with its talons that the venom was forced to flow."

"It is not as you say," added still another, "for the kite was at no fault there. It ate what it was accustomed to eat, doing no more than was natural to it. The serpent that spit out the poison was to blame."

"You are wrong," said the fourth, "for the serpent was guiltless. The maidservant was the guilty one, because she failed to cover the milk when she was carrying it from the market."

"You are all in error," stated Sindibad. "The maidservant was blameless in the matter, for no one had ordered her to cover the milk; nor was the kite to blame, because it was eating what it was supposed to eat; nor was the serpent at fault, because it was in the power of another; nor was the host blameworthy, because no man can taste every dish he has prepared."

"All these men say naught," the king then told his son. "You explain to me whose was the blame."

"None of these was to blame," the prince replied, "for the hour in which each was to die was at hand."

As soon as the king heard this, he cried, "God be praised that He didn't let me execute my son! And you, Sindibad, have done well and you have placed us under great obligation to you; but you know whether the prince has any more to learn. Teach it to him, and you shall have a noble reward."

"Sire," said Sindibad, "I know nothing at all that I haven't taught him, and I believe that there is nothing else in the world. No one is wiser than he."

"Is what Sindibad said true?" the king asked the wise men who stood around him.

They replied that no one should speak evil of what seems good.

"He who does what is good," stated the prince, "deserves a fine reward. I shall tell you who knows more than I."

"Who?" asked the king.

THE TALE OF THE TWO WISE CHILDREN, OF THEIR MOTHER, AND OF THE YOUNG MAN[62]

"Sire, they tell a story of two boys, one four years old, the other five, both blind and deformed. Now everybody says that these are wiser than I."

"How were these wiser than you?" the king asked.

"I understand that a man who never heard of a beautiful woman that he didn't lose his wits over her, found out about one. He sent his manservant to tell her that he was madly in love with her. Now that woman had a four-year-old boy. When the messenger returned with her reply that she was willing to do whatever he pleased, the master went to her.

'Wait a bit,' she told him, 'and I shall feed my son. Afterwards I shall come to you.'

'Do what I want to first,' insisted the man, 'and feed the child after I have gone.'

'If you knew how wise he is, you would not say that,' replied the mother.

She stood up, placed a pot upon the fire, poured rice in and cooked it. She took a little in a spoon and put it before the child, who wept and said, 'Give me more, for this is just a little!'

'You want more?' she asked.

'More,' he replied.

And he asked her to pour some olive oil from the bottle. And he wept all the while and was not silent. Then he cried out, 'Woe unto you! I never saw anyone crazier than you and so witless!'

'How do I seem crazy and witless to you?' the man asked.

'I am only weeping for myself,' said the boy. 'Why do my tears trouble you? I am perfectly sane. My father used to help me to all the rice I could eat when I wept for it. The crazy, witless, and stupid one is he who leaves his country, abandons his children and his possessions and relatives to go awhoring across the earth, seeking what will harm him, weakening his body, and falling beneath God's wrath.'

When the child told him all this, the fellow realized that he was wiser than his father. He went to him and hugged him and cuddled him.

'Upon my word,' he exclaimed, 'you are right! I didn't believe that you were as wise as you are. I am astonished at all you have said to me!'

And he repented and made amends."

THE TALE OF THE FIVE-YEAR-OLD BOY AND OF THE COMPANIONS WHO INTRUSTED THEIR MONEY TO AN OLD WOMAN

"And, Sire, I shall tell you about the five-year-old child."

"Then tell it," said the king.

"I heard it related that three companions[63] were in a market and that they left it wealthy. The three took the road, and it happened that they found lodging with an old woman to whom they gave their money to hold for them.

'Do not give it to any one of us unless we are all present,' they admonished her.

'Very well,' she replied.

After that they went into an orchard that the old woman owned to take a bath in a tank that was there. Two of them spoke to the other, saying, 'Go to the old woman and tell her to give you a comb so we can comb our hair.'

'My friends,' he told the old woman, 'want you to give me the money, for we want to count it.'

'I shan't give it to you,' she replied, 'until all of you are together as you agreed.'

'Come to the door,' he told her. 'Speak to the old woman,' he called to his friends, 'for she wants to know if you sent me.'

'Get it and give it to him,' they called.

So she went and gave him the money. He took it and went away, thus deceiving his companions.

Now when they noticed that he was delaying, they went to the old woman and said to her, 'Why are you delaying our friend?'

'I have given him the money you ordered me to give him,' she told them.

'Woe unto you!' they cried. 'We didn't tell you to give him the money, but only a comb!'

'He has taken away the money you gave me,' she said.

They cited her before the judge and told him their grievance. Now the judge decreed that the old woman must pay back the money, since she had understood the agreement. Weeping, the old woman met a five-year-old child.

'Why are you crying?' the child asked her.

'I am crying because of my bad luck and over the misfortune that has befallen me, and for heaven's sake let me be!'

The child walked along behind her until she told him why she was crying.

'I will give you some advice about this trouble you are in, if you will give me a coin to buy dates with,' he said. 'Go back to the judge and tell him that you have the money, and say, "Judge, tell them to bring their friend, and unless they do, I shan't return the money to them, not until they appear together. That is the way they made the agreement with me."'

She returned to the judge and told him just what the child

had advised. The judge realized that someone had counseled her.

'For goodness' sake, old woman,' he said, 'please tell me who it was that advised you.'

'A little boy I met in the street,' she answered.

The judge had a search made for the child, and they brought him to him.

'Did you advise this old woman?' the judge asked.

'I advised her,' the boy replied.

Then the judge was very much attracted by the child and he adopted him and sheltered him for his wise counsel."

They were all pleased with the tale of the five-year-old.

THE TALE OF THE SANDALWOOD MERCHANT AND OF THE OTHER MERCHANT[64]

"How was that?" asked the king.

"Sire, they tell the tale of an old man. They say that once there was a very rich merchant in sandalwood. He inquired in what land sandalwood was most costly and he traveled there.

Now he was passing near a goodly city and he said to himself, 'I shall not enter this city until dawn.'

While he was in that spot, a damsel went by leading a flock to pasture, and when she saw the caravan, she inquired what he was bringing and from whence he came. The damsel then went to her master and told him how there were merchants at the village gate who were carrying a great supply of sandalwood.

This man went and cast what sandalwood he had into the fire, and the merchant smelled the smoke of sandalwood and was alarmed.

'Look to your loads so that they won't catch fire,' he said, 'for I smell sandalwood smoke.'

They looked over the loads and found nothing. Then the merchant arose and went to the shepherds to see if they had gotten up.

Now the man who was burning the sandalwood came to the merchant and said to him, 'Who are you? How is it going with you? What merchandise are you carrying?'

'We are sandalwood merchants,' replied the merchant.

'Alas, good man,' cried the man, 'we don't burn anything here except sandalwood!'

'How can this be?' asked the merchant. 'I inquired, and they told me that there was no land where sandalwood was more expensive and where they valued it so much.'

'The one that told you that,' said the man, 'wanted to deceive you.'

Then the merchant began to complain and curse. He made great moan.

At this the man spoke to him and said, 'Upon my word, I feel sorry for you! Since things are like this, I will buy it from you and will give you what you ask. Bring it and turn it over to me.'

The merchant handed it over to him, and the man took the sandalwood and carried it to his house. Now when morning came, the merchant entered the town and took lodging in the house of an old woman. He inquired of her as to what sandalwood was worth in the city.

'It is worth its weight in gold,' she told him.

The merchant was filled with regret when he heard it.

'Good man,' said the old woman, 'the people of this city are deceivers and dirty-dealers, and no stranger ever comes here whom they don't cheat. Watch out for them!'

The merchant went to the market place and came upon some men who were shaking dice. He stopped and watched them.

'Do you know how to play this game?' one of them asked him.

'Yes, I know how,' he replied.

'Well, sit down,' said one, 'but let the condition be understood that the loser shall be obliged to do whatever the winner requires.'

'I agree,' said the merchant.

So it was that they played, and the merchant lost.

'You must do what I command,' said the winner.

'That is true,' said the merchant.

'Well,' said the man, 'I command you to drink all the water of the sea and not to leave even a single drop.'

'Very well,' replied the merchant.

'Provide pledges that you will do it,' the man insisted.

The merchant went along the street and met a man who had only one eye.

'You stole my eye! Go before the judge with me,' cried the man.

The old woman, his hostess, said to the man with one eye, 'I am his pledge in the matter, and I will bring him before the judge for you tomorrow.'

And then she said to the merchant, 'Didn't I warn you that the men of this town were wicked and evil-natured? Well, since you refused to believe what I warned you about in the first place, don't be slow to believe what I shall now tell you.'

'Upon my word,' answered the man, 'I shall never wander from your advice and your orders.'

'Know that they have as master an old blind man who is very wise,' the woman told him. 'They all join him at night, and each tells him everything that he has done during the day. Now if you could join them in disguise while they tell him what each of them did to you, you would hear what the blind man advises them to do to you, for it is certain that all of them will tell everything to the blind man.'

The merchant therefore went to that place and, disguised, went in with them and sat down and heard everything they told the blind man. Now the first said that he had bought the sandalwood from the merchant under such terms that he would pay the merchant what he asked.

'You acted like a stupid fellow,' cried the blind man. 'How would you like it if he demanded fleas, half of them female and half male, some blind and some lame, some green and some scarlet, and the rest red and white, with only one normal?'

'That will not occur to him,' replied the man. 'He won't ask for anything except money.'

The one who had shaken dice with the merchant then stood up and said, 'I gambled with that merchant and I told him that he must do what I commanded him to do. I told him to drink up all the water of the sea.'

'You did as badly as the other,' said the old man. 'How would you like it if the other should say, "I agreed to drink up all the water of the sea, but you be certain that no river nor stream flows into it. Then I shall drink. See if you can do that!"

'I met this same merchant,' said the other, rising to his feet, 'and saw that he had eyes like mine. I said to him, "You stole my eye. Don't leave until you give it to me, or what it is worth."'

'You were not wise, nor did you know what you were doing,' said the old man. 'How would it be for you if he should say,

"Pluck out the one you still have, and I shall pluck out one of mine, and we shall see whether they are alike or not?"

'Now if you do this, you will be blind and the other will have one eye, and you won't have any. You would lose more than he.'

When the merchant heard this, he was pleased, and he took it all to heart. He returned to his lodgings and told the old woman everything that had happened to him, and he considered that he had been well advised by her. He rested that night in her house and at daybreak he saw the one who had bought his sandalwood.

'Give me the sandalwood,' the merchant demanded, 'or what you agreed to give.'

'Tell me what you want for it,' replied the man.

'Give me,' said the merchant, 'a bushel of fleas full up, half females and half males; half red and half green; and half scarlet and half yellow; and half white.'

'I'll give you money,' said the man.

'I want nothing but the fleas,' insisted the merchant.

The merchant had the man summoned before the judge. The judged ordered the man to give him the fleas, and the man told him he could have his sandalwood. Thus the merchant recovered his sandalwood by the counsel of the old blind man.

'Fulfil the bargain you made with me,' said the one who had played dice, 'that you will drink up all the water in the sea.'

'All right,' replied the merchant, 'provided that you watch all the rivers and streams that enter the sea.'

'Let's go before the judge,' said the man.

'Is this the way it stands?' asked the judge.

They said that it was, and the judge ordered, 'You see that no more water flows into the sea, and he states that he will drink it up.'

'It is impossible,' said the man.

Then the judge ordered him to release the merchant from his promise.

'Give me my eye,' cried the one-eyed man, who happened along just then.

'Very well,' answered the merchant. 'You remove the eye you have, and I shall take this one of mine out, and we shall see if they match each other. We shall weigh them, and if they are alike, it is yours; and if it isn't yours, pay me what the law requires.'

'What do you say?' asked the judge.

'How can I take out my eye,' he said to the judge, 'since then I would have none?'

'Well, he demands what is right,' stated the judge.

The man said he didn't care to take it out, and he withdrew charges against the merchant. And this is the way it happened to the merchant with the men of that city.

Sire, I told you this tale so that you would know the tricks of the world."

THE TALE OF THE WIFE, THE CLERK, AND THE FRIAR[65]

"How was that?" asked the king.

"I heard about a woman," began the prince, "whose husband had to go away on business. She then sent to tell the clerk[66] that her husband was out of town and he should come to her house that night. The clerk came and entered the house. Now, when midnight approached, the husband returned and knocked at the door.

'What now?' asked the clerk.

'Go and hide in that room until daylight,' she ordered.

Her husband came in and went to bed. When dawn came, the woman arose and went to a friar, her confidant, and told him what had taken place, and begged him to bring a monk's habit with which to disguise the clerk who was in her house.

The friar went and said to her, 'Where is So-and-So?'

'He hasn't gotten up yet,' she told him.

The friar went in and asked the husband how he was, and he stayed there until the clerk was dressed. Then the friar said, 'Excuse me, for I must be off.'

'Go, and God keep you,' the husband replied.

Now as the friar came abreast of the room, out came the clerk dressed as a friar and accompanied him to his monastery.

And Sire, I gave you this tale for the sole reason that you might distrust women, who are evil; for the sage says that if the earth should change into paper, and the sea into ink, and its fish into pens, they would not be able to set down the wickedness of women."

And the king commanded her to be roasted in a dry cauldron.[67]

NOTES

1 T. Benfey, *Pantschatantra* . . . . (Leipzig, 1859), Vol. I.
2 Emma E. Kiefer, *Albert Wesselski and Recent Folktale Theories*, p. 19.
3 For a complete classification of these tales according to standard motif-indexing see Stith Thompson, *Motif-Index of Folk-Literature*, and John E. Keller, *Motif-Index of Mediaeval Spanish Exempla*.
4 A complete listing of the occurrence of such tales in the folktales of the Appalachian Mountains would be too long for inclusion here. For a lengthy discussion of folktales in all parts of the world see Stith Thompson, *The Folktale*, and for examples of some of the mountain tales themselves see Richard Chase, *The Jack Tales* (Cambridge, Mass., 1951). In one section of this book, "Appendix and Parallels," written by Herbert Halpert, a number of tales are discussed and their oriental sources mentioned.
5 Variously called *The Book of Sindibad, The Book of the Seven Sages, The Seven Wise Masters, The Seven Viziers, Sendebar*.
6 For further treatment of the theory of diffusion from India see M. Menéndez y Pelayo, *Orígenes de la novela*, I, 27-113; V. Chauvin, *Bibliographie des ouvrages arabes* . . ., II, 1-8, and VIII, 1-4; A. González Palencia *Historia de la literatura arábigo-española*, 2nd ed., pp. 338-48; D. Comparetti, *Researches Respecting the Book of Sindibad* (London, 1882), pp. 1-69; N. M. Penzer, *The Ocean of Story*, X, 207-243.
7 Some of the stories were carved on the stupas at Sanchi, Amaravati (now on the grand staircase of the British Museum) and at Bharut. At Bharut the titles are inscribed above the *Jatakas*. These carvings may date from as early as 400 B.C.
8 A suggestion that the account about Barzuyeh might have been an invention may be found in Max Müller, "On the Emigration of Fables," *Contemporary Review*, XVIII (1870), 577.
9 Abdallah-ben-Almocaffa was born (ca. A.D. 725) of Persian parents and reared in the religion of Zoroaster. His father, whose Persian name was Daduyeh, held the position of receiver of revenues at Fars. When it was discovered that he had embezzled public funds, he was put to torture, and one of the results of this punishment was a shriveled hand, whence the name al-Mocaffa, 'the Shriveled.' The son, Abdallah, was a man of great culture and ability. Converted to Islam while relatively young, he gained high renown as a writer and an intellectual, and must have been exceedingly well-qualified to make a faithful translation of the Persian version of *Kalilah wa Digmah*. Some time after his translation was made, he became involved in a conspiracy against the caliph and was executed (ca. 760). See entry under Abdallah-ben-Almocaffa in *Encyclopedia of Islam*.
10 For a lengthy discussion of John of Capua's version, translated from the Hebrew, see Joseph Derenbourg, *Deux versions hebraïques du livre de Kâlilâh et Dimnah*. Menéndez y Pelayo gives a concise treatment of this matter in *Orígenes*, I, 32.
11 V. Chauvin, II, ix gives the *stemmata* of *Kalilah wa Digma*.
12 For a description of the only extant manuscript of this mediaeval Spanish version see *El libro de los engaños*, ed. by John E. Keller (Chapel Hill, 1953).
13 Petrus Alphonsi, whose Hebrew name was Rabbi Moseh Sephardi, was born in Huesca, Spain, in 1062 and was baptized in 1106. His royal patron was King Alfonso of Aragon, known as the Battler. The *Disciplina Clericalis*, according to a statement in its prologue, was written a few years after his conversion and baptism. He is also known for his *Dialogues* in defense of the Christian faith against the Hebrew (available in Migne, *Patrologia Latina*, CLVII, 535-671). See also *The Jewish Encyclopedia*, II, 377.
14 The influence of the *Disciplina Clericalis* was phenomenal, especially

in the twelfth, thirteenth, and fourteenth centuries, and later and less directly in the Renaissance. The *Gesta Romanorum*, *The Canterbury Tales*, and *The Decameron* are only three of the many books that drew material from it. Hilka and Söderhjelm have described and classified sixty-three separate Latin manuscripts of this work in their comprehensive study of the Latin versions in *Acta Societatis Scientiarum Fennecae*, Vol. XXXVIII, No. 4. Other writers who made use of the tales in the work of Petrus Alphonsi were Odo of Cheriton, Etienne de Bourbon, Nicholas de Bozon, Clemente Sánchez, and Jacques de Vitry. The best available edition of the Latin text is that of Hilka and Söderhjelm, *Die Disciplina Clericalis des Petrus Alfonsi* (Heidelberg, 1911). A. González Palencia published *Disciplina Clericalis* (Madrid, 1946), reproducing the text according to Hilka and Söderhjelm, together with those tales from the *Disciplina Clericalis* translated into Spanish by Clemente Sánchez. He lists also the names of authors who borrowed from Petrus Alphonsi, according to Chauvin (IX, 44).

15 According to Comparetti (p. 5), the Persian Musa probably wrote his version of *The Book of Sindibad* in Arabic. The Syriac version, considered to be the immediate source of the *Syntipas*, contains a prologue in which the Syrian translator states that he used a text written by Musa.

16 The Greek and Spanish versions are the most closely related of all the extant renditions. The former contains twenty-five stories, three of which are not found in the latter. The last tale in the Spanish text, "The Tale of the Woman, the Clerk, and the Friar," is found in no other rendition. The Hebrew version has twenty-two tales, seven of which are common to both the Spanish and the Greek; the *Sindibad-nâmah* numbers twenty-five, seven of which appear in the Greek and Spanish, four in the Hebrew; the Arabic version, represented by *The Thousand and One Nights*, has twenty-nine tales, sixteen of which are found in the Spanish and the Greek. For a listing by title of all the stories in the seven members of the eastern branch see Comparetti (p. 25); for eastern and western branches see Chauvin (VIII, 5-217).

17 A. H. Krappe, "The Seven Sages," *Archivum Romanicum*, VIII, 386-407; IX, 345-65; XVI, 271-82; XIX, 213-26.

18 For a discussion of the Latin prose *Dolopathos* of Johannis de Alta Silva (Haute-Seille), see U. T. Holmes, Jr., *History of Old French Literature*.

19 These three Spanish representatives of the western branch appear in González Palencia's *Versiones castellanas del "Sendebar"*. All are presented in their complete form except *Historia lastimera del Principe Erasto*, which is represented by only the four tales that do not appear in any of the other three sixteenth-century Spanish texts.

20 The *Era Española*, 'Spanish Era,' was based upon the calendar of Caesar, which began thirty-eight years before the Christian computation. Aragon gave up reckoning by the *Era* in 1350, Castile in 1383.

21 See J. E. Keller, *Motif-Index*, sections J and K.

22 Fadrique was closely connected with Alfonso's court and must have shared his brother's interest in Arabic writing. Among the works translated from the Arabic under the direction and patronage of King Alfonso X were treatises on the Mohammedan faith, chess, law, and the famous lapidaries. See Américo Castro, *España en su historia* . . . (Buenos Aires, 1948) pp. 83-96, 209-10, 213-14, 298-99, 310-12, 349. For a discussion of Alfonsine translations from the Arabic see Evelyn S. Proctor, *Alfonso of Castile*.

23 The Spanish text contains numerous syntactical usages of great interest and antiquity and certain words not recorded in other Old Spanish works; furthermore, the manuscript, written in one hand, with the emendations set down probably a full century later in another, illustrates many changes that occurred during that period of time. The original hand records some three hundred readings which were altered, deleted, or paraphrased by a later scribe.

24   The Spanish text is the only one that mentions this king; moreover, it is the only version that names him king of Judea. Most list the country as India or China, or name no country. The identification of Alcos has not been verified. Some have suggested Chosroes of Persia (ruled A.D. 531-79); others Kûrush or Kai Kûrush of India.

25   This is *The Book of Exempla by A.B.C.*, known in Spanish as *El libro de los enxienplos por a.b.c.*, by Archdeacon Clemente Sánchez. Two manuscripts exist: the Paris manuscript is intact, but the Madrid text begins only in the middle of the listings under the letter *C*. F. Morel-Fatio published an edition of the first part from the Paris manuscript, beginning with *A* and ending in *C*, in *Romania*, VII (1870), 481-526. Pascual de Gayangos edited the entire manuscript of Madrid from the middle of *C* to the end in *Biblioteca de Autores Españoles*, LI, 443-552. No complete critical edition of this great collection exists.

26   For the most complete discussion of the *exemplum* used in didactic writings see J. Welter, *L'exemplum dans la littérature religieuse et didactique du Moyen Age*.

27   St. Ambrose in one of his letters wrote: "*Exempla subjicit, ut facilius suadeat; quia cui verba satis non faciunt, solent exempla suadere.*" (Migne, *Patrologia Latina*, XVII, Ch. X, col. 145, vers. 15).

28   Of interest are the words of the famous bishop, Jacques de Vitry, urging the use of *exempla* in sermons. "With strange and polished words laid aside," he wrote, "we must turn our minds to the teaching of the rude and the uncultured who are moved rather by clear *exempla* than by authoritative or profound maxims." (T. F. Crane, *The Exempla of Jacques de Vitry*, pp. xli-xliii.)

29   The collection of Clemente Sánchez represents the apogee of the Spanish tradition of *exempla*.

30   Alfonso Martínez de Toledo in his *El Corbacho* relates four tales from his experience, or so he reports. These tales deal with wiles practiced by wives upon their husbands, wiles identical, almost, with some of the tales in the *Disciplina Clericalis* and some of the sermon stories of the collection of Clemente Sánchez. It is quite possible, even probable, that if Spanish women of the fifteenth century, women known by Martínez de Toledo, Archpriest of Talavera, practiced these deceits upon their unsuspecting spouses, they heard about such wiles in sermons. Opponents of the *exemplum* saw this possibility and accused the preachers of abetting the very sins they decried.

31   Wycliffe in 1381 wrote scornfully about friars who used holy days to preach fables which distracted people from their devotions, and he criticized with equal severity the subject matter employed by these same friars, calling their *exempla* mendacious jokes and fraudulent fables. To him the duty of preachers was plain: "The theologian must sow the true Scripture, not exploits and earthy chronicles." Mosher in *The Exemplum in the Early Religious and Didactic Literature of England* (p. 17) gives the Latin for these lines. His study of the *exemplum* is of great value to scholars in this field.

32   In Canto XXIX (The Temple Classics, Edinburgh, 1937, pp. 356-58) Dante devoted these lines to the matter:

"Such fables Florence in her pulpit hears,
Bandied about more frequent than the names
Of Bindi and of Lapi in her streets.

. . . .

The preacher now provides himself with store
Of jests and jibes; and, so there be no lack
Of laughter, while he vents them his big cowl
Distends, and he has won the meed he sought."

33   The general tone of the councils in regard to the *exemplum* was the same. The Council of Salzburg focused attention upon the *exempla* themselves, criticizing, however, preachers who employed them for unseemly reasons; at Sens, Milan, and Bordeaux decrees were issued against mora-

lized tales, and priests who used them were threatened with suspension. For a complete picture of the actions taken by the councils, see them re-recorded in Mansi, *Sacrorum Conciliorum nova et amplissima Collectio* (Venice, 1759-98), Vol. XXXII, Sess. XI, col. 946 and col. 1199; Vol. XXXIV, col. 9 and col. 1579. See also J. Th. Welter, *L'exemplum dans la littérature religieuse et didactique du Moyen Age*, p. 453.

34 Menéndez y Pelayo (*Orígenes*, I, 35) cites from Argote de Molina *Nobleza de Andalucía*, II, fol. 180, the following letter written by San Pedro Pascual, Bishop of Jaén (14th century) to Christians incarcerated by the Moors of Granada: "And friends, be certain that you will better spend your time and your days reading this book [?] and hearing it, than in telling and hearing fables and romances of love and of other things they have written about animals and birds that they assert used to speak in other times. And it is certain that they never spoke: these stories were written for the sake of pointing moral lessons. And if any good lesson is found in them, there are also found many deceptions and snares for the body and the soul."

35 Not a great deal is known about the life of Prince Fadrique. Spain's great *Enciclopedia Universal Ilustrada* gives him no separate listing, but mentions him under that of his brother, Alfonso X; Ballesteros (*Historia de España*, III, 168) says that the king, his brother, had him put to death in Burgos because he was fearful that a rebellion would be raised and because he had learned by means of astrology that a close relative would lead it. Fadrique sided with Alfonso's hated wife, Queen Violante, when she refused to accept her husband's choice of an heir in Sancho, their second son. With the assistance of Fadrique and other nobles, Violante fled to the court of her brother in Aragon, taking her grandchildren, the children of her deceased eldest son Fernando, with her so as to remove them from the danger threatened by Sancho. It is almost certain that for his part in the flight of the queen Fadrique was executed in 1277 by order of Alfonso. Subsequent events indicate that Violante was wise in deciding to leave the realm. Sancho deposed his father (although he later restored to him some degree of authority before the king's death in 1284) and ascended the throne as Sancho IV.

36 Ferdinand III (ruled 1217-52) gained the sobriquet *El Santo*, 'The Saint,' through his activities against the Moors. The actual turning point of the reconquest took place in the time of Alfonso VIII at the Battle of the Plains of Tolosa (1212); Ferdinand, however, had no small part in the long struggle that followed. Cordoba fell to his armies in 1236 and Seville in 1248. After this, Moorish dominions were limited to the small Kingdom of Granada, which finally succumbed to Ferdinand and Isabella in 1492. Ferdinand III was proud of his nation and of his language, which was Castilian. This pride was passed on to his children, especially to Alfonso the Learned. Ferdinand married Beatrice of Suabia (1219) by whom he had ten children, among them Alfonso and Fadrique. It was during Ferdinand's life that Castilian began to come into use in official documents. During the reign of Alfonso Latin was entirely discontinued by decree and Castilian became the official tongue. The learned king saw the propaganda value of a national literature and realized how beneficial it would be if the laws of the land, national history, and the arts and sciences were rendered understandable to his subjects. Literary and intellectual activity at his court was rivaled nowhere else in the thirteenth century except possibly in Sicily.

37 The text reads *Plogo e tovo por bien que aqueste libro de aravigo en castellano para aperçebir a los engañados e los asayamientos de las mugeres*. The later scribe emended *engañados* to *engaños*. The word *e* does not mean 'by,' but as there are many scribal errors in the text it is possible that *e* was meant to be written *de*, 'by.' The line was translated in line with this reasoning.

38 This false accusation, listed as Motif Number K2111, Potiphar's wife (Thompson, *Motif-Index*), is best known through Scripture (*Genesis* 39:7-10). It is paralleled in the legend of Bellerophon, in the *Iliad*, and in the

ancient Egyptian tale of the Two Brothers. Many occurrences of this theme appear in distant parts of the world and are probably not dependent upon the Biblical account.

39 See Thompson, K978, Uriah letter, for occurrences of this motif. See also J. Keller, *Motif-Index of Mediaeval Spanish Exempla*. Motif numbers hereafter cited in Keller refer to this classification of medieval Spanish tales. The Uriah letter motif occurs also in *El corbacho* and in *El libro de buen amor*.

40 See the unpublished doctoral dissertation (University of North Carolina) by Walter R. Heilman, "The Pastourelle Theme in the Early Spanish Drama," for a lengthy treatment of the situation in which a clever woman escapes the seductive advances of a nobleman. Keller, J816.4.

41 Thompson, Keller, J1154.1. The occurrence of the theme in *The Thousand and One Nights* is the most famous in literature.

42 Keller, J2175.4.

43 Thompson, Keller, N383.2.

44 Keller, K1517.1.

45 This same tale was used in *El libro de los enxienplos por a.b.c.* and in the *Disciplina Clericalis*.

46 Thompson, Keller, G405.

47 Thompson, Keller, N381.

48 Thompson, Keller, D12. This story is obscure as to meaning in the Spanish, probably because of poor copying or failure to make a correct translation from the Arabic. A check of other versions does not clear it up, for no identical account is found in the others. The motif of the changed sex is present in *The Thousand and One Nights*, but the confusing interchange in *The Book of the Wiles of Women* seems to be peculiar to it. The point of the story may be that the demon, now pregnant, cannot assume his former shape, and hence the prince must also remain a woman. The prince appeals the case, in view of the facts, and is permitted to become a man again.

49 Keller, K1544 and P325. The story is found also in *El libro de los enxienplos por a.b.c.* and *El Cavallero Zifar*.

50 Thompson, Keller, K1351. In *Disciplina Clericalis* and *Libro de los enxienplos por a.b.c.*

51 Keller, J514.4.

52 Thompson, Keller, B331.2. Found also in *Calila e Dimna*.

53 Thompson, Keller, K1543.

54 Keller, J1781.8.

55 The conclusion of this story is not germane to the point which is supposedly being made, for at the beginning the woman had said "I trust in God who will shelter me from your wicked privy-counselors, as he protected a lion on one occasion." At the end she says ". . . just as he helped the robber against the ape."

56 Thompson, Keller, N346. Found also in *Calila e Dimna*.

57 Keller, J2301.2.

58 Thompson, Keller, J2071.

59 Keller, K1227.

60 *Carofoja*, 'clovepink,' raises a question. Clovepink is a flower, and it may seem difficult to imagine fire being struck from rubbing a flower upon a wood like sandalwood. The point in this concept seems to be that two cold substances if rubbed together engender heat, and both sandalwood and the clovepink appear to be considered cold. The idea is odd, but no more so than many folk beliefs about plants. I derive *carofoja* from Latin *caryophyllam*. Another etymology might be Greek Kárphos, but if this is used the matter of the two cold substances is lost.

61 Thompson, Keller, N332.3.

62 Keller, J122.1.
63 Thompson, Keller, J1161.1. Used also in *Libro de los enxienplos por a.b.c.*
64 Keller, H1129.10.1.
65 Keller, K521.6.
66 The title of this story names a *clerigo*, 'priest' or 'lay clerk.' In the body of the story, however, this character is named the *abbad*. The word abbad, in addition to its meaning of 'abbot,' has also the connotation of 'priest' or, for that matter, any religious. Since a real abbot would have been clothed in his habit, he would not have needed to borrow one, but a clerk certainly would have.
67 The fate of the wicked stepmother varies in the several versions: she is hanged in Nachschebi's Persian version; she is cast into the sea with a stone tied to her foot in *The Seven Viziers* rendition; she is pardoned in the *Mischlè Sendebar*; in the *Syntipas* she is forced to ride through the streets with her head shaved, followed by two criers who announce her evil deeds.

SELECTED BIBLIOGRAPHY

ARABIC
Habicht, Maximilian. *Tausend und Eine Nacht, Arabisch nach Handschrift aus Tunis hrsg.* Breslau: Hirt, 1825.
Scott, F. *The Seven Visiers* (1800), reproduced by W. A. Clouston. *The Book of Sindibad; or, Story of the King, his Son, the Damsel, and the Seven Viziers. From the Persian and Arabic.* Glasgow: Cameron, 1884.
GREEK
Boissonade, Joseph E. *Syntipas et Cyri filio Andreopuli narratio et codd.* Paris: Bure frères, 1828.
Eberhard, Alfred. *Fabulae Romanenses Graece conscriptae ex recensione et cum adnotationibus.* Leipzig: Teubner, 1872.
HEBREW
Sengelmann, Heinrich von. *Das Buch den sieben weisen Meistern aus dem hebräischen und griechischen zum ersten Male übersetzt und mit literarhistorischen Vorbemerkungen versehen.* Halle: Lippert, 1842.
PERSIAN
Brockhaus, H. *Die sieben weisen Meister von Nachschabi, Persisch und Deutsch.* Leipzig, 1845.
Falconer, Forbes. *Analytical Account of the Sindibad-namah, or Book of Sindibad.* London: (Journal of the Royal Asiatic Society of Paris), Vols. XXXV, XXXVI.
SPANISH
Bonilla y San Martín, Adolfo. *Libro de los engaños e los asayamientos de las mugeres.* Biblioteca Hispánica. Barcelona-Madrid, 1914.
Comparetti, Domenico. *Researches Respecting the Book of Sindibad.* (The Folk-Lore Society), No. IX. London: Stock, 1882.
———. *Ricerche intorno al libro di Sindibâd.* (Atti del Istituto Lombardo), 1869; 2nd ed., Florence, 1896.
González Palencia, Ángel. *Versiones castellanas del "Sendebar."* (Consejo Superior de Investigaciones Científicas). Madrid-Granada, 1946.
Keller, John Esten. *El libro de los engaños.* (University of North Carolina Studies in the Romance Languages and Literatures). Chapel Hill, 1953.
SYRIAC
Baethgen, Friederich von. *Sindban, oder die sieben weisen Meister Syrisch und Deutsch.* Leipzig, 1879. Translated into French by Macler, Paris, 1903.

EDITIONS OF THE WESTERN BRANCH
Chauvin, Victor. *Bibliographie des ouvrages arabes ou relatifs aux Arabes.* Liège: H. Vaillant-Carmanne; Leipzig: Harrassowitz, 1904. (Vol. VIII, 1-215 contains bibliography of Sindibad through 1922, Eastern and Western branches: editions, studies, articles, dissertations, etc.).

GENERAL BIBLIOGRAPHY

Adams, Nicholson B. *The Heritage of Spain.* New York: Henry Holt, 1943.
Alighieri, Dante. *The Paradiso.* (Temple Classics). Edinburgh, 1937.
Amador de los Ríos, José. *Historia crítica de la literatura española*, Vol. III. Madrid: J. Rodríguez, 1863.
Ballesteros, Antonio. *Historia de España y su influencia en la historia universal.* 10 vols. Barcelona: Salvat, 1918-41.
Barlaam et Josaphat, ed. F. Lauchert. Romanische Forschungen, VII (1893), 32-402.
Beal, Samuel. *The Fo-sho-hing-tsan, a Life of Buddha.* Oxford: Clarendon, 1883.
Bédier, Joseph. *Les Fabliaux, étude de littérature populaire et d'histoire littéraire du Moyen Age.* Paris: Bouillon, 1895.
Benfey, Theodor. *Pantschatantra: fünf Bucher indischer Fabeln, Märchen und Erzählungen.* Leipzig, 1859.
Burke, U. R. *A History of Spain from the Earliest Times to the Death of*

Ferdinand the Catholic. 2 vols. 2nd ed. London: Longmans, Green, 1900.
Calila y Dimna, ed. J. Alemany Bolufer. Madrid: Librería de los Sucesores de Hernando, 1915.
Campbell, Killis. *A Study of the Romance of the Seven Sages* with Special Reference to the Middle English Versions. (Johns Hopkins University doctoral thesis.) Reprinted from the Publications of the Modern Language Association of America, Vol. XIV, No. 1, 1-107.
Carter, Minnie Luella. "Studies in the Scala Celi of Johannes Gobii Junior." (Unpublished doctoral thesis, University of Chicago, 1928.)
Chapman, Charles E. *A History of Spain.* New York: Macmillan, 1918.
Crane, Thomas F. *The Exempla of Jacques de Vitry.* (Publications of the Folklore Society, No. 26). London: Nutt, 1890.
Crónica de los reyes de Castilla, ed. D. Cayetano Rosell. *Biblioteca de Autores Españoles,* LXVI. Madrid: Librería de los Sucesores de Hernando, 1919.
Derenbourg, Joseph. *Deux versions hébraïques du livre de Kâlilâh et Dimnah.* Paris: 1881.
Dunlop, John C. *History of Fiction.* London: Bell, 1889.
Enciclopedia Universal Ilustrada Europeo-Americana. 70 vols. + 16 supplementary vols. Barcelona: Hijos de Espasa, 1930-44.
Encyclopedia of Islam. 4 vols. Leyden-London, 1913-36.
González Palencia, Ángel. *Historia de la España musulmana.* 2nd ed. Barcelona: Editorial Labor, 1929.
―――. *Historia de la literatura arábigo-española.* 2nd ed. Barcelona: Editorial Labor, 1945.
Harduin, J. *Acta Conciliorum.* Paris, 1714.
Harold, A. F. *The Life of Buddha according to the Legends of Ancient India,* translated from the French by Paul C. Blum. New York: Boni, 1927.
Heilman, Walter R. "The Pastourelle Theme in the Early Spanish Drama." (Unpublished doctoral dissertation, University of North Carolina, 1952.)
Hitti, Philip. *History of the Arabs from the Earliest Times to the Present.* 5th ed. New York: Macmillan, 1951.
Holmes, Urban T., Jr. *History of Old French Literature.* New York: Crofts, 1937.
Hurtado, Juan, and A. González Palencia. *Historia de la literatura española.* 6th ed. Madrid: S.A.E.T.A., 1949.
Isidore of Seville. *Opera Omnia.* Rome, 1862; J. P. Migne, *Patrologia Latina,* vols. 81-4; *Etymologies,* ed. W. M. Lindsay. 2 vols. Oxford: Clarendon, 1911.
Jacobs, Joseph. *History of the Æsopic Fable.* London: Nutt, 1889.
Jewish Encyclopedia. 12 vols. NewYork-London: Funk and Wagnalls, 1901-05.
Juan Manuel, Infante of Castile. *El Conde Lucanor,* ed. Hermann Knust pub. by Adolf Birch-Hirschfeld. Leipzig: Seele, 1900.
Keller, John Esten. *Motif-Index of Mediaeval Spanish Exempla.* Knoxville: The University of Tennessee Press, 1949.
Kiefer, Emma E. *Albert Wesselski and Recent Folktale Theories.* Indiana University Publications, Folklore Series No. 3. Bloomington, 1947.
Komroff, Manuel. *Tales of the Monks from Gesta Romanorum.* New York. Tudor, 1928.
Krappe, A. H. "Les sources du *Libro de los Exemplos,*" *Bulletin Hispanique* XXXIX (1937), 5-54.
Lane-Poole, Stanley. *The Moors in Spain.* New York: Putnam, 1890.
Lecoy de la Marche, A. *La chaire française au Moyen Age.* Paris: Renouard-Laurens, 1886.
Martínez de Toledo, A. *El corbacho,* ed. Lesley B. Simpson. Berkeley: University of California Press, 1939.
Menéndez y Pelayo. *Orígenes de la novela.* Vol I. Santander: Consejo Superior de Investigaciones Científicas, 1948.
Migne, J. P. *Patrologiae Cursus, Series Latina.* 221 vols. Paris: Migne, 1844-64.

Millares Carlo, A. *Historia de la literatura española hasta fines del siglo XV.* "Clásicos y Modernos," No. 5. Mexico, 1950.
Misrahi, Jean. *Sept Sages.* Paris: Libraire E. Droz, 1933.
Mosher, Joseph A. *The Exemplum in the Early Religious and Didactic Literature of England.* New York: Columbia University Press, 1911.
Nicole de Bozon. *Les contes moralisés,* ed. Paul Meyer and L. Y. Smith. Paris: Sociéte des Anciens Textes Français, 1889.
Paris, Gaston. "Les contes orientaux dans la littérature française du Moyen-Age." (3rd essay in *La poésie du Moyen-Age,* II ser.) Paris, 1887.
Penzer, N. M. *The Ocean of Story*: being C. H. Tawney's translation of Somadeva's *Kathā Sarit Sāgara.* 10 vols. London: 1923 ff.
Petrus Alfonsi. *Disciplina Clericalis,* ed. Alfons Hilka and Werner Söderhjelm. Heidelberg: Winter, 1911.
———. *Disciplina Clericalis,* ed. A. González Palencia. Madrid-Granada: Consejo Superior de Investigaciones Científicas, 1948. (This edition follows that of Hilka and Söderhjelm and gives those stories from Petrus Alfonsi's work borrowed and translated into Spanish by Clemente Sánchez in *El libro de los enxienplos.*)
Proctor, Evelyn S. *Alfonso of Castile, Patron of Literature and Learning.* Oxford: Clarendon, 1951.
Salazar, Pedro. *Monarquía de España.* 2 vols. Madrid: Ulloa, 1770.
Sánchez, Clemente. *El libro de los exemplos,* ed. P. Gayangos. Biblioteca de Autores Españoles LI, Madrid, 1952; *Romania* VII (1878), 481-526.
Thompson, Stith. *The Folktale.* New York: Dryden, 1951.
———. *Motif-Index of Folk-Literature*: a classification of narrative elements in folktales, ballads, myths, fables, mediaeval romances, exempla, fabliaux, jest-books, and local legends. 6 vols. FF Communications Nos. 106-109, 116, 117. Helsinki, 1932-36. Also Indiana University Studies Nos. 96-97, 100, 101, 105-106, 108-110, 111-12. Bloomington, 1932-36.
Welter, J. Th. *L'exemplum dans la littérature religieuse et didactique du Moyen Age.* Paris-Toulouse: 1927.
Wright, Thomas. *A Selection of Latin Stories from Manuscripts of the 13th and 14th Centuries.* Percy Society Publications. Vol. 8. London: Richards, 1843.

The Department of Romance Studies Digital Arts and Collaboration Lab at the University of North Carolina at Chapel Hill is proud to support the digitization of the North Carolina Studies in the Romance Languages and Literatures series.

www.ingramcontent.com/pod-product-compliance
Lightning Source LLC
Chambersburg PA
CBHW020422230426
43663CB00007BA/1277